MANUEL A. RODRIGUEZ

America's Seashore

TIM THOMPSON

Wonderlands

Prepared by the Special Publications Division
National Geographic Society, Washington, D.C.

TIM THOMPSON

AMERICA'S SEASHORE WONDERLANDS

Contributing Authors:
  TOM MELHAM, H. ROBERT MORRISON, WHEELER J.
  NORTH, CYNTHIA RUSS RAMSAY, SUZANNE VENINO
Contributing Photographers:
  MATT BRADLEY, STEPHEN FRINK, STEPHEN J.
  KRASEMANN, TIM THOMPSON

Published by THE NATIONAL GEOGRAPHIC SOCIETY
GILBERT M. GROSVENOR, *President*
MELVIN M. PAYNE, *Chairman of the Board*
OWEN R. ANDERSON, *Executive Vice President*
ROBERT L. BREEDEN, *Vice President,*
  Publications and Educational Media

Prepared by THE SPECIAL PUBLICATIONS DIVISION
DONALD J. CRUMP, *Editor*
PHILIP B. SILCOTT, *Associate Editor*
WILLIAM L. ALLEN, *Senior Editor*

Staff for this Book
SEYMOUR L. FISHBEIN, *Managing Editor*
CHARLES E. HERRON, *Illustrations Editor*
MARIANNE RIGLER KOSZORUS, *Art Director*
ALICE JABLONSKY, *Project Coordinator and Senior Researcher*
TEE LOFTIN, *Researcher*
PATRICIA F. FRAKES, RALPH GRAY, ALICE JABLONSKY,
  PAUL MARTIN, SUZANNE VENINO, *Picture Legend Writers*

Contents

ELIZABETH ANN BRAZEROL, PAMELA BLACK TOWNSEND,
  Editorial Assistants
CAROL ROCHELEAU CURTIS, STUART E. PFITZINGER,
  Illustrations Assistants
JOHN D. GARST, JR., VIRGINIA L. BAZA, D. MARK
  CARLSON, JOSEPH F. OCHLAK, ISAAC ORTIZ, NANCY
  S. STANFORD, KEVIN QUINN STUEBE, *Map Research
  and Production*

Engraving, Printing, and Product Manufacture
ROBERT W. MESSER, *Manager*
GEORGE V. WHITE, *Production Manager*

GEORGE J. ZELLER, JR., *Production Project Manager*
MARK R. DUNLEVY, DAVID V. SHOWERS, GREGORY
  STORER, *Assistant Production Managers;* MARY A.
  BENNETT, TIMOTHY H. EWING, *Production Assistants*

LORI E. DAVIE, MARY ELIZABETH DAVIS, ANN DI FIORE,
  ROSAMUND GARNER, BERNADETTE L. GRIGONIS,
  VIRGINIA W. HANNASCH, NANCY J. HARVEY, JOAN
  HURST, LINDA JOHNSON, ARTEMIS S. LAMPATHAKIS,
  KATHERINE R. LEITCH, ANN E. NEWMAN, CLEO E.
  PETROFF, VIRGINIA A. WILLIAMS, *Staff Assistants*

J. W. HARCHICK, *Indexer*

Sanderlings skitter before advancing surf. Pages 2-3: Big Sur headlands reflect a Pacific sunset. Page 1: A brown pelican rests in the Florida Everglades.

The Wonderlands

An Introduction by Wheeler J. North

WE KNOW IT as a wonderland of summer pleasures, fresh breezes, lazy clouds, blue water curling white, flinging shells and wisps of weed onshore. What will the next wave bring? A child wonders, a poet wonders. A scientist, too. The shore and its fringing sea always hold promise of little surprises, the unexpected.

I have studied the restless margins of the oceans for more than 35 years. Often my work takes me undersea in scuba gear, amid fluorescent animals that glow like little orange or red candles. I may swim by hot springs that send silvery streams of bubbles chasing each other to the surface, or encounter opossum shrimp hovering like layers of mist just above the seafloor.

California's undersea kelp forests, so useful to man, became my specialty. Studying the problem of pollution in kelp, I visited some of the most awesome sewer outfalls in the world—somber and, at times, surprising places.

One day the city of Los Angeles shut down its discharge so that a group of us could survey its giant outlet 200 feet down in Santa Monica Bay. The bottom was carpeted in black, a shroud of decaying organic matter; hand movements or fin kicks sent inky clouds rolling up. I had the eerie feeling of gliding through a ghostly cemetery at midnight. Suddenly I noticed up ahead the gleam of what looked like white marble pillars rising out of the gloom. As I drew closer, to my amazement the pillars proved to be a colony of sea anemones, their pure white bodies crowned

---

As bold as its colors, the garibaldi darts out like a warning flare when strangers near its nest. Here it highlights a rocky California bed studded with spiny sea urchins, hung with green kelp and pink coralline alga. Its spunk made the "ocean goldfish" easy prey for collectors. Today California protects it and honors it as the state saltwater fish.

STEPHEN FRINK

with frilly tentacles. I had first studied anemones years earlier at Cambridge in England. But those were only a few inches high. Here in Santa Monica Bay grew monsters as big around as telephone poles, some as tall as I.

In the funereal atmosphere these magnificent specimens were like old friends, reassuring me that my surroundings were not entirely a hostile wasteland. The memory of those snow-white columns rising from the dark sediments will remain with me always.

People often wonder at the contrasts in our seashores. Why are there no forests of giant kelp along our Atlantic seaboard, ask friends and students. And why does California lack anything like Florida's magnificent coral reefs? Why are there great chains of barrier islands along our Atlantic and Gulf coasts but not the Pacific?

Barrier islands, undersea forests, and other major coastal features arose from events in the geologic past and are sustained by processes that mold today's world. As Ice Age glaciers retreated and sea levels rose, sandy barrier islands formed along Atlantic and Gulf shores that had broad, gently sloping coastal plains. Our Pacific edge, in the main, is a cliff coast.

Giant kelp, *Macrocystis*, the glory of the California submarine forest, probably originated in temperate waters of the Southern Hemisphere, occurring on both sides of South America. During the Ice Age, surface waters off Central America cooled on the Pacific side, but remained tropical in the Atlantic. According to one theory, giant kelp migrated north across the cold-water "bridge." Cold currents and rich nutrients sustain the forest today. The kelps along our cold northeastern coast are short-statured seaweeds that also grow in Europe.

Reef-building coral animals, on the other hand, flourish only in tropical waters. The tepid Gulf Stream allows corals to proliferate in the east at latitudes that are far too cold on western shores. The result is massive, beautiful coral growth in Florida, but not in California.

In the sea, as on land, what grows in a given place depends a lot on the character of the ground. But there's a curious difference. Not much grows on rocky land. Plants and animals of the seashore, however, thrive on rock. Soft bottom shifts under the force of waves; plants cannot easily colonize unstable terrain. On such a surface, or substrate, lush plant growth develops in the calm of bays, estuaries, and lagoons—the wetlands, bounteous nursery of the seaboard.

Life at the edge must cope with waves, wind, heat, and cold. The rise and fall of the tides poses another challenge: Many creatures of the shore must spend part of their lives out of water, often under a desiccating sun. Members of the tidal community are adapted in a pattern of vertical zoning; species that can survive the most exposure live at the highest levels.

Some periwinkle snails dwell up in the spray zone, wetted only by the highest tides or by storm waves. I remember as a graduate student taking periwinkles out of the spray zone for study. Thinking I would do them a favor, I dropped them into a bowl of seawater. Not long after, I noted with dismay that every one of them had crawled up the container's side, out of the water. And there they remained until they died. The lesson I learned was that these periwinkles can move to drier levels if they get too much water—but they are not adapted to seeking moisture. The little they need comes to them, with extreme high tide or storm spray. One must, as it were, force seawater on them to keep them alive.

My periwinkles lasted a month before desiccation killed them. Some species last much longer in total dryness. There's the tale of the museum periwinkle that broke loose from its card and crawled away—some two years after the "dead" snail had been put on display!

Just under the spray zone, animals with cone-shaped shells may appear: the little volcano cones of the barnacles that are attached to the rocks, and the limpets with their coolie-hat shells. Just below are the dark spiky clusters of the mussel beds. Lower down the variety increases. You may have to move mounds of seaweed and pry into crevices and under rocks to see

everything there is to see. Many of the plants are the wrong colors, appearing as red, black, brown, pink, almost anything but green. Some single-cell plants live within the flesh of animals. The plants photosynthesize more food than they need; the animals use the surplus. In symbiotic exchange the animal tissues protect the plants from being consumed by microscopic grazers.

Animals here may begin life as swimmers or drifters and later become attached to one spot. How do they collect enough food to survive? Some, called filter feeders, strain out plant and animal cells passing by in the current. Oysters and mussels are stationary filter feeders.

When water temperature, sunlight, and dissolved nutrients all become favorable at the same time, population explosions of plant cells may occur, adding so many billions that the water changes color from blue to turbid green, yellow, brown, or red. The latter two hues contain the microfloras of the fearsome red tides, with their deadly toxins. Swimming in a red tide may bring no harm. But eating a filter feeder, such as an oyster, that has concentrated the toxins in its flesh can be disastrous. Red tides tend to occur in late spring and summer. Hence the adage: Avoid oysters in months without an R.

Among one group of seashore animals the species protect their outer surfaces with pointed spicules or spines. They are known as echinoderms, spiny skins, and include sea stars, sea cucumbers, and sea urchins. The latter can move about on the tips of their spines, like a child on stilts; cucumbers are not nearly as spiny.

Like many other kinds of life at land's end, the cucumber resembles its terrestrial namesake in form, though not in substance. The sea cucumber may be long and slender, but it is animal, not vegetable. The sea hare has the silhouette of a rabbit, but none of its agility; the sea hare is a slug—very sluggish. Coastal life includes sea lice and sea cows, sea palms and sea lettuce. The stinker sponge stinks; the do-not-touch-me sponge will blister your hands. The lion's paw is harmless, a scallop with knuckle-like bumps on its shell. But avoid the lion's mane; it is the largest of all jellyfish, known to measure eight feet across. Its name derives from its shaggy tentacles, and they are loaded with poison that can cause pain and discomfort. Sherlock Holmes alleged much worse in *The Adventure of the Lion's Mane.*

A scuba diver may truly become an inhabitant of the oceanic realm, even if ever so briefly. While terrestrial animals tend to flee from humans, most marine animals have not yet developed fear of the bubbly monster. Consequently, when waters are clear, divers observe multitudes of curious, often beautiful animals hovering in forest foliage or threading mazes of intricately branching corals. Sometimes fishes are so tame they'll take food from a diver's hand. Off Catalina Island I once took a picture of my diving companion kissing a little harbor seal on the nose.

"We have lingered in the chambers of the sea, by sea-girls wreathed in seaweed red and brown." Like T.S. Eliot's Prufrock, I have lingered in those chambers, some 5,000 hours all told, often wreathed in seaweed. So far the mermaids have eluded me. But I keep my mask unfogged, for there are wonders still to see.

And yet, having spent a professional lifetime studying human influences on the sea, I am well aware of how vulnerable our seashore wonderlands are, how slowly our understanding grows of the ecology that sustains them. We have harvested mindlessly, washed toxins into the waters, built on shifting sands, destroyed wetlands or disfigured them beyond succor.

Perhaps no one has done more than the late Rachel Carson to focus concern on the abuse of our environment—or to excite our sense of wonder at the "primeval meeting place" of land and sea. Excerpts from her work appear at the beginning of each of the five major chapters that follow, with acknowledgments on page 196.

Here is a sampling of her witchery—words from the closing evocation of *The Edge of the Sea*, written in her cabin along the Maine coast:

"Now I hear the sea sounds about me; the night high tide is rising, swirling with a confused rush of waters against the rocks below my study window. Fog has come into the bay from the open sea, and it lies over water and over the land's edge, seeping back into the spruces and stealing softly among the juniper and the bayberry. The restive waters, the cold wet breath of the fog, are of a world in which man is an uneasy trespasser; he punctuates the night with the complaining groan and grunt of a foghorn, sensing the power and menace of the sea.

"Hearing the rising tide, I think how it is pressing also against other shores I know—rising on a southern beach where there is no fog, but a moon edging all the waves with silver and touching the wet sands with lambent sheen, and on a still more distant shore sending its streaming currents against the moonlit pinnacles and the dark caves of the coral rock.

"Then in my thoughts these shores, so different in their nature and in the inhabitants they support, are made one by the unifying touch of the sea. For the differences I sense in this particular instant of time that is mine are but the differences of a moment, determined by our place in the stream of time and in the long rhythms of the sea. Once this rocky coast beneath me was a plain of sand; then the sea rose and found a new shore line. And again in some shadowy future the surf will have ground these rocks to sand and will have returned the coast to its earlier state. And so in my mind's eye these coastal forms merge and blend in a shifting, kaleidoscopic pattern in which there is no finality. . . .

"On all these shores there are echoes of past and future: of the flow of time, obliterating yet containing all that has gone before; of the sea's eternal rhythms—the tides, the beat of surf, the pressing rivers of the currents—shaping, changing, dominating; of the stream of life, flowing as inexorably as any ocean current, from past to unknown future. For as the shore configuration changes in the flow of time, the pattern of life changes, never static, never quite the same from year to year. Whenever the sea builds a new coast, waves of living creatures surge against it, seeking a foothold, establishing their colonies. And so we come to perceive life as a force as tangible as any of the physical realities of the sea, a force strong and purposeful, as incapable of being crushed or diverted from its ends as the rising tide."

9

THE BREAKERS AT OLYMPIC NATIONAL PARK, NEAR LA PUSH, WASHINGTON; ART WOLFE/APERTURE PHOTOBANK

"The sea's method on a rocky coast is to wear it down by grinding, to chisel out and wrench away fragments of rock, each of which becomes a tool to wear away the cliff. . . . The breakers on such a coast have a different sound from those that have only sand to work with—a deep-toned mutter and rumble not easily forgotten." RACHEL CARSON

10

The Northwest

By Cynthia Russ Ramsay

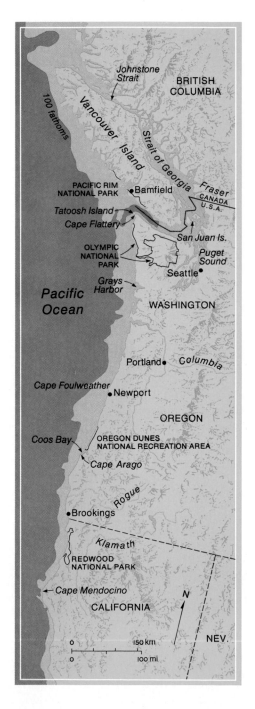

OUT OF THE OCEAN'S DARKNESS they came, speeding toward the gray-green waters of the shore. At first only their triangular dorsal fins were visible. But when they came into the shallows, sleek black-and-white torpedo shapes broke the surface as the swimmers rolled over and wriggled to scratch themselves on the pebbles below. Killer whales had come to one of the unique "rubbing beaches" of British Columbia's Vancouver Island, roiling the water with their antics and play. Watching these great beasts leap into the air virtually at one's feet is an uncommon experience. Ahead of me lay many more, for wonders are commonplace along these shores.

Consider the grunion—the only fish known to leave the sea and lay its eggs in sand. On the moonlit beaches of southern California, hordes of silvery grunions writhe in their mating dance. Offshore, fertile waters nurture the fastest growing marine plant in the world—giant kelp—forming golden undersea forests that sway with the perpetual surges of the sea. On land, the tallest of living things, the coast redwoods, survive along the fog-shrouded edge of California and southern Oregon—and nowhere else.

Along this coast, and northward, stretch the unmatched driftwood beaches—mammoth logs and root tangles abraded by wind, salt, and wild surf into silvery, surreal sculptures. Jostling masses of seals and sea lions blanket rocks and beaches. In the spring a rush of flowers brushes the offshore islands with color; nesting colonies settle in and the small, sharp cries of thousands upon thousands of baby birds begging for food mingle with the ceaseless sounds of the surf.

The landscape creates its own spectacles.

From Vancouver Island's surf-washed parks to the redwood coast of northern California, driftwood-strewn beaches and steep cliffs break the long fetch of wild Pacific waves. Wet northwest winds slake dark evergreen forests, and the tides flood rocky pools teeming with invertebrate life. Whales and seals, foraging bears, salmon bound for spawning stream or open ocean, and millions of ravenous birds range the shores and bordering sea.

Bold headlands bear the brunt of waves rolling in unimpeded from Asia; the sea batters itself into spray sometimes a hundred feet high, bursting through gaps and blowholes of its own making. Geysers of surf, cliff-hung beaches, forested inlets, and a myriad of living things as well—all these I saw as I traveled from Vancouver Island to California's murky redwood coast and on a second journey southward to sunnier shores.

From slippery seaweeds with such graphic names as Turkish towel and feather boa to brilliantly colored sea slugs, from the buck-toothed California sheephead, a fish that changes its sex, to the gigantic gray whales, the Pacific edge musters an extraordinary roster of life.

This rich assemblage owes much to the phenomenon of upwelling. As ocean currents flow south along the coast, wind patterns and the earth's rotation combine to deflect surface water away from shore. To replace it, cold, nutrient-rich water wells up from below, replenishing the surface supply of nitrates and phosphates from the residue that has drifted down to the depths. The minerals foster the growth of diatoms and dinoflagellates, microscopic, single-celled plants that have been called the most important single foodstuff in the ocean. During a seasonal bloom of this phytoplankton—plant wanderers—the cells may number from a hundred million to a billion or more to the cubic meter.

In contrast to the other two coasts, the Pacific shore perches on the edge of a narrow continental shelf; waters as deep as 800 feet lie less than half a mile offshore. In the Atlantic and in the Gulf of Mexico the coastal plain slopes gently out to sea, extending the continental shelf a hundred miles or more in most places. Huge slabs of the earth's crust collide at the Pacific margin, making it one of the most unstable, earthquake-rocked regions of the world. Over millions of years the jolting, buckling, and uplifting has fringed the coast with craggy grandeur.

My discovery of the Pacific shores began at Johnstone Strait between Vancouver Island and mainland British Columbia. Evergreens, dense and dark, press in on the horizon, but the solemn beauty takes second place to the spectacle of the swift and incredibly powerful killer whale, *Orcinus orca*. Whale-watchers converge here, and the sight of dorsal fins knifing through the water brings gasps of excitement and anticipation, for killer whales are highly sociable mammals that travel, feed, and rest in close-knit family groups called pods.

Skipper Jim Borrowman, who takes visitors out on his boat, once witnessed an unforgettable sight: the birth of an orca. "The mother immediately pushed the baby to the surface for air, and then she and other members of the pod took turns holding the baby there," recalls Jim. They lifted with their flippers or butted with their heads, keeping its blowhole out of the water. It was clear the newborn didn't know how to breathe. But within an hour the calf was diving. "Then," Jim adds, "the whole pod, with the baby in the middle, swam slowly past the boat as if they were parading the baby and showing it off."

Killer whales range the world's oceans, but Johnstone Strait sustains a particularly large resident population with its abundance of cod, herring, and the salmon funneling to and from the spawning streams of the Fraser River system. With 150 orcas in 13 separate pods, the strait is an ideal study site, and it is here that researchers have made some startling discoveries.

Observers reached a milestone when they learned to tell the animals apart by individual markings on the dorsal fin and by variations in the black-and-white pattern just behind the fin. Soon after, researchers began to perceive family ties—and how strong and lasting they are. More surprising was the discovery that each pod communicates in its own dialect. The sounds, consisting of whistles, nasal grunts, and strident screams, vary from group to group, and a pod can be identified by its version of the calls.

Up to 25 feet long and six tons in weight, their huge jaws studded with terrible teeth, killer whales were once maligned as man-eaters. The record shows not a single human fatality from a killer whale attack, but these wolves of the sea are indeed fearsome predators, hunting down seals, sea lions, and whales with deadly efficiency when fish are scarce. A scientist who watched a pod feeding in the Arctic saw one orca clamp its jaws on a gray whale and thrust it a third of the way out of the water—a feat of strength, considering the victim weighed about ten tons!

Sometimes the pods of Johnstone Strait come together in conclaves of up to a hundred animals, the young churning the water with their acrobatics. They breach, catapulting into the air; they lobtail, slapping the surface with their flukes; and they spy hop, rising straight up, half out of the water, like periscopes. The adults, more sedate, simply become more loquacious. In Puget Sound, another community of resident killer whales begins similar meetings with more elaborate greeting ceremonies. Richard Osborne, research director of the Whale Museum on San Juan Island, has watched the arrivals rush toward each other head-on and wriggle and rub against one another repeatedly. Afterward, all the animals, even the adults, join a boisterous playtime that may last for hours.

Differences in behavior, like the varied dialects, suggest that each community of killer whales has evolved its own traditions and perhaps passes them on from one generation to the next. This seems to be saying that culture shapes the life-styles of these animals—to me a rather startling notion.

More surprises lay in store for me at the Friday Harbor Laboratories on San Juan, where biologists study such creatures as the tiny mollusks that live in the pore spaces of coarse sand, the ribbon worm that paralyzes its prey with a poisoned dart in its proboscis, and the sea squirt so transparent you can look inside and see the heart pumping blood. Many jellyfish are also transparent and readily reveal their insides, which are little more than a tube and mouth that hang from the center of the round or bell-shaped body and lead directly to the stomach. Sixty-five jellyfish species float in the fertile waters surrounding the San Juan Islands—far more variety than anywhere else in the United States.

"Some are smaller in diameter than a sequin, others are more than three feet, but if it's umbrella-shaped and moves by pulsating, it's a jellyfish," said Claudia Mills, who has studied them for more than a decade. They are called medusae because their long, curling tentacles recall the hideous snake-haired Medusa of Greek mythology, and they have kept the same general shape for the last 600 million years, according to fossil remains traced in rock.

"Medusae have a simple but effective body plan that hasn't changed much over time," said Claudia as she led me to a tall, cylindrical tank filled with running seawater. There we could observe these creatures whose lineage ranks among the oldest in the animal kingdom. Several individuals of the species *Aequoria victoria* were sweeping the water with long tentacles; their bodies looked like glistening crystal dinner bells. Small prey jellyfish were added to the tank. After a while an *Aequoria*'s tentacle snared a victim and immobilized it with stinging capsules called nematocysts. At the lightest touch these capsules explode and inject a toxin into the victim. The tentacle, easily three feet long, coiled the prey to the margin of the bell, where the morsel was rolled into the transparent stomach.

Claudia has no trouble netting specimens, for the waters teem with life. In the Puget Sound area the fertility comes from silt dumped by Ice Age glaciers, augmented by runoff from mountain streams. Tides and currents surging past the San Juan Islands churn this debris into the upper layers. There the microscopic plants and sunlight perform their special alchemy, upon which nearly all life in the sea depends.

The glaciation that shaped Puget Sound also notched Vancouver Island with spectacular fjords. Their calmer waters are quite unlike the wild tormented surf pounding the headlands on the open ocean. Boating in the area of Barkley Sound on the southwest corner of the island allowed me to experience a little of both, but the balmy July days spared me the vicious storms and smothering fogs that have marked this stretch of coast as a "graveyard of the Pacific."

Only a soft drizzle descended the morning I set out in a motorized Zodiac raft with John Oliver, a California marine biologist studying the feeding tactics of gray whales in the Barkley Sound area. For some unknown reason about 50 of 18,000 gray whales fail to make the complete migration from the nurseries of Baja California to summer feeding grounds in the Arctic. Instead the dropouts tarry along the coasts of Vancouver Island, Washington, Oregon, and northern California, eating small crustaceans found in soft ocean sediments, as well as tube worms living on sandy bottoms. John, a diver, has followed the animals underwater to study the bottom-feeding technique. The gray whale, he said, turns on its side and, with the flukes fanning back and forth, sucks in its food—silt and all—through the side of its huge mouth. Before swallowing, the whale probably uses its tongue, which weighs about 3,000 pounds, to sluice water and most of the sand out through the baleen strips hanging like a curtain from its upper jaw.

Suddenly a slate-gray mound broke the monotony of the small waves. We heard the whoosh of the whale's breath, like a deep, heavy sigh, before we saw the vapor plume of its blow. The whale bobbed near the surface for three breaths, then flipped its great flukes up and disappeared. A few minutes later the pattern was repeated, and so it went for the next two hours. We were ignored, but on other days whales have come right up to John's boat—sometimes pushing it gently. Once an animal aimed a blow that wet everyone aboard. It seemed quite deliberate. "What was worse was its breath, which smells like rotten eggs," said John.

We had been cruising open water along the island's outer coast. Evergreens pruned by wind and salt spray rose like tattered flags and everted umbrellas on the cliff ledges. High up on the rocks, where only storm waves fling their spray, a marine lichen called *Verrucaria* encrusted the surface in an irregular glossy black band, tracing perfectly the ocean's highest reach. In the protected waters inside Barkley Sound trees grew right down to the high-water mark—their growth trimmed in a sharp, even line where salt water had nipped the buds and young leaves.

On another day Anne Bergey, biological technician at the Bamfield Marine Station on Vancouver Island, and I were motoring toward some beds of eelgrass, a flowering, seed-bearing plant that roots only in sheltered water. Along the way we caught sight of a black bear and her two cubs on a cobble beach. The sow was turning rocks to get at the small purple shore crabs underneath. Anne nosed the Boston whaler into a narrow channel. Ahead, floating on the dark surface, were dense patches of eelgrass aswarm with all manner of living things. Anne lifted a blade about three feet long. "Look," she said, "the white pinpoint dots are the calcareous

casing of tube worms; there's a microscopic animal inside." Tiny globs of jelly lay on the blade; these, Anne noted, were egg capsules of the snails known as bubble shells.

"Herring also come up to lay their eggs on the eelgrass," she continued. "The sea lions follow right behind; then you see them with their whiskers covered with the clear shiny beads of herring roe." Flatworms crawl along the leaves, and tiny crustaceans cling to them. Snails and sea slugs lay their eggs on eelgrass, sea anemones grow on it, crabs crawl on it, and sea stars decorate it. Jellyfish drift and small fish dart among the leaves, and clams burrow down among the roots in the mud.

Such dense populations are not unusual along the coast, but little compares with the extraordinary concentrations found in the rocky zone where tides batter the community with breakers, flood it, and then, retreating, expose it to blistering sun. Paradoxically it is in this intertidal realm, so unstable and so harsh, that marine plants and animals crowd every available spot on the rocks and fill every tidepool with a glorious profusion of life.

The seaweeds, small and large, including the kelps with their broad, leathery blades, cope with the turbulence by anchoring themselves to rock by rootlike holdfasts. The sea palm, one of the smaller kelps, thrives in pounding surf. The rubbery stalks and drooping blades, bending and whipping like a palm tree on a hurricane coast, always indicate the roughest water.

"Just as long as the mussels keep away from their holdfasts, the sea palms will do fine," said Robert T. Paine, a marine biologist at the University of Washington who has made Tatoosh Island his laboratory for some 17 years. The seaweed and the mollusk compete for space. The sea palm can gain a foothold where heavy waves rip away the mollusks; occasionally the alga establishes itself on top of mussels. In calmer water, the mussels win out. (Continued on page 21)

Head fixed in a familiar beachcomber stance, a hungry black bear on Vancouver Island flips the stones with sharp curved claws. Not a picky eater, the bear searches the shore for crabs, dead fish, anything edible. Into the mouth of Barkley Sound (below) drifts a lone escapee from a log boom. On this day the Pacific reflects its name; on other days the ocean roars. British Columbia's temperate winters and drenching rains nurture conifer forests that yield nearly half of Canada's timber harvest.

Killer whales at play rub bellies and backs on a pebble-bottomed playground off Vancouver Island. The amenities here in Johnstone Strait also include a wealth of cod, herring, and salmon, enough to sustain 13 resident pods. Unlike the sharp-toothed, white-bibbed hunters, the much larger gray whale (right) mines its meals in the muck. In this rare photograph of feeding behavior the whale has just sucked in a mouthful of mud. The silt filters out through the baleen plates—the strainers that hang from the upper jaw—and the morsels remain: crustaceans, perhaps some small fish. A leisurely diner, the gray whale may spend hours at a sitting,

interrupting regularly for a breather at the surface just a few feet above. After calving season ends, most gray whales migrate from Baja California to the Bering Sea; some cut short their northward travels to summer at a few sites off southern Canada and the U.S. coast.

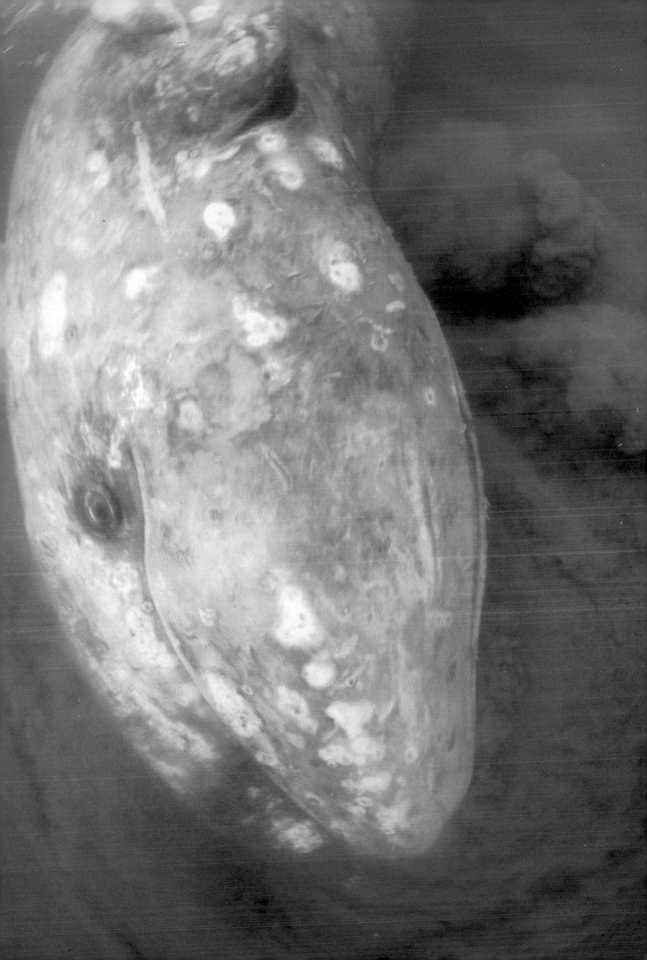

Tatoosh Island, at the mouth of the Strait of Juan de Fuca, boasts one of the lushest, most unspoiled arrays of intertidal life in the world. Ferocious surf, tricky currents, and the Coast Guard—which maintains the Tatoosh lighthouse—keep away casual roamers and souvenir hunters. Through their studies here Paine and his students have added significantly to our understanding of intertidal ecology.

"One of the more obvious things about the intertidal is that plants and animals are not randomly distributed," Paine told me as we sped toward the island on a fishing vessel. "Generally speaking, they are segregated in zones or horizontal bands that depend, in part, on how long they can survive out of water and how well they tolerate strong wave action." The zones begin in the higher places moistened only by spray and range down to reefs exposed only at the lowest tides.

Paine and the students head for Tatoosh on those days of highest and lowest water. They occur just after new moon and full moon, when earth, moon, and sun are aligned; combined gravitational forces pull on the earth and its oceans along the same plane, producing the extremes called spring tides. The name suggests "springing" waters, not the springtime of the year. Every lunar month has its spring tides—and also its neaps, the days of minimum tidal range. These occur during the quarter moons, when the forces of sun and moon pull at right angles, counteracting one another. For observing intertidal life, spring tides are best; when the tide runs out on those days, it exposes the low intertidal zone and leaves clear placid pools in places usually churned by breaking waves.

Only boaters and the hardiest hikers on Vancouver Island's West Coast Trail get close to Tsusiat Falls, whose waters sometimes plummet into a freshwater pool—and occasionally into the sea. During winter months fierce surf may combine with highest tides to surge over the gravel beachhead, obliterating the pool. Built as a lifesaving route for shipwrecked seamen, the grueling 44-mile trail winds through sodden forests, up and down steep cliffs, and along log-piled beaches in Pacific Rim National Park.

Near the island we scrambled into a Zodiac, and Paine steered through the surf and the rocky shallows. Glaucous-winged gulls stood their ground nearby, braying in a discordant chorus as we hauled the raft high up on the gravel—high enough to put it beyond the reach of the spring tide. "The gulls get up in the air fast enough when a bald eagle comes by," said Paine, "for they know it is looking for birds that can't fly."

We packed our gear up a steep trail cut into a cliff and came to a plateau overgrown with pink fireweed and white cow parsnip. From there we could look across the channel to Cape Flattery and the long, lonely beaches of Washington's Olympic Peninsula.

No humans inhabit Tatoosh these days, for the Coast Guard lighthouse is fully automated, but the island plays host to summer colonies of birds. During the afternoon, while the tide was up and flooding the areas we wanted to explore, we made the time memorable by watching the nesting common murres and pelagic cormorants. Row by row they lined high ledges on the precipitous southwest side of the island. As soon as the cormorants came in from the sea, they spread their wings to dry, for the oil glands of these swift swimmers do not waterproof their feathers very well. Most of them stood facing the wall, like captives, because the narrow ledges left no room for their tails. The murres, on the other hand, kept their eyes to seaward, and at some sighting only these plump birds could interpret, they took off one after the other, a black-and-white squadron in perfect line formation.

On this coast the lowest tides of summer tend to occur early in the morning—a time of frequent fogs. "That's an enormous boon to plants and animals because the fog provides some protection against dehydration, sunburn, and scorching," said Paine as he nimbly led us from one algae-draped rock to the next. We were crossing a rocky platform, leaping over pools festooned with bizarre and beautiful creatures.

In a draw two red blobs caught my eye. One was a sea squirt, or tunicate—a gelatinous animal that lives inside a thick tunic and filters microscopic food from the water with twin siphons. One siphon draws the water in; the other squirts it out. The baggy creature, stuck to one spot, looks like a simple life form, but its tadpole-like larva contains a notochord—a stiffened rod, evolutionary forerunner of the backbone. Adult sea squirts lose both the rod and the ability to swim, yet they belong to the Phylum Chordata along with all the other vertebrates, including fishes—and humans.

The second red animal I had spotted was a sponge, another sessile, or stationary, filter feeder. The sponge filters bacteria from water siphoned through its myriad pores. A large part of the pool was occupied by what looked like round pincushions. These were the sea urchins, covered with spines of a rich purple hue, and somewhere in each bristling being were versatile tube feet which the animal uses not only for moving about but also for grasping kelp to eat. Five shiny teeth scrape and chew the food, with a rig of levers and muscles known as Aristotle's lantern—in honor of the philosopher of ancient Greece who described sea urchins as lantern-shaped. Surprisingly mobile, these animals often gather in greedy herds that destroy large patches of kelp, resulting in urchin barren grounds.

Most elegant were the giant green anemones, like pale dahlias in full bloom on the ocean floor. But these flowers of the sea are carnivorous animals. The sea anemones rarely move about; like their free-floating relatives, the jellyfishes, they paralyze prey with toxins in tiny sacs that bulge along petal-like tentacles. "They like to be in channels where they can feed on things crushed and washed off by the waves," said Paine, dropping an empty mussel shell into one of the anemones. Its tentacles instinctively curled around the shell, then slowly released the indigestible piece.

"Anemones just roll with the punches," Paine observed. "When food is plentiful, they grow in size. When things are bad, they shrink. Size does not indicate age. We don't know how old these creatures are. Some of these anemones might be a thousand years old, or older."

Exploring the intertidal, you either skid and wobble along on rocks slippery with kelp, or you head for the gritty surface of barnacle-covered rocks. The barnacle begins life as a free swimmer. Then, ending its larval stage, it cements itself to the rocks of the upper intertidal. Standing on its head, the barnacle surrounds itself with limy plates, and—when the tide is up—kicks food into its mouth with feathery appendages.

When the tide retreats, the barnacle retracts into its shell, closing the plates as it rides out the dry spell. Thus the barnacle can hold the high ground of the intertidal. In the lower zones the rocks are blanketed with mats of mussels. Many intertidal animals seek out the mussel beds, for the cracks and crevices there provide refuge from the surf and from predators. Like birds in a tree, the resident limpets, chitons, and snails cruise outside to feed, creating a barren zone around the mussel bed where the animals have grazed down the fleshy algae.

Mussels, which fasten to rocks with silky elastic threads spun out of a foot, are the favorite food of the ochre sea star, the most voracious predator of the intertidal. (Starfish is a much more familiar, but somewhat imprecise name for these invertebrates; scientists prefer sea star.) With its hundreds of tube feet, the sea star pulls the mussel shell apart. Then it quickly everts its stomach into the gap to digest the soft insides. These orange or purple-hued marauders limit the spread of the mussel beds down the intertidal, for the lower a mussel goes, the longer it's submerged, and the greater the risk of becoming a meal for the starfish. The sea star tends to shun the higher zones where it faces the danger of dehydration, but the bivalved mussel keeps itself from drying out by clamping shut the two parts, or valves, of its shell. One of the commonest sights on Tatoosh was a rock literally plastered with the five-armed sea stars. The mussels were above, beyond reach—at least until the return of high water put the prey within range again.

One of Paine's experiments has been to see what happens when sea stars are removed from an area. The site is now called "the glacier," because the mussel beds have been slowly advancing down the shore. And as the mussels increase they crowd out the sea cabbage, whose large, thick blades provide food and cover for a diverse group of sea creatures.

It was from such studies that Paine developed his concept of the "keystone" species. The ochre sea star is one. While feasting on mussels, the predator exerts a key influence on the makeup of the entire community. "Much of the complexity of this shore is due to this sea star because it helps keep mussels down and creates living space for others," said Paine. "Competition for space and what mediates it is what intertidal ecology is all about."

In some intertidal communities even such a placid, passive species as the aggregating anemone vies for space—with its own kind. This greenish anemone, fringed with bright pink or lavender tentacles, has two forms. One of them lives a solitary existence, reproducing sexually with eggs and free-swimming larva. The other lives in aggregations that reproduce asexually by cloning. The animals simply tear themselves in half. If an individual from another colony comes too close, the aggregation will deploy stinging cells against the intruder, which responds in kind. When researchers mixed separate clone groups together, they eventually resegregated themselves. How the anemones can tell the difference, no one knows.

From Tatoosh I proceeded south along the foggy, blustery beaches of Olympic National Park. This corner of northwest Washington is drenched in fall and winter, when the Pacific high pressure system weakens and wild storms from the Gulf of Alaska move in. More than a hundred inches of rain a year nurture a luxuriant forest with ferns, mosses, and moldering logs, with lichens and tangled vines everywhere. The park also protects 57 miles of rocky and sandy beaches, with the dark forest rising just behind them. Often not a sound can be heard except for the surf and the cries of gulls. Sometimes a Columbia black-tailed deer will burst out of the sylvan edge and add its lithe silhouette to the shore.

Farther south I strolled the pocket beaches of Oregon, scallops of seashore set off by promontories, cliffs, and sculptured sandstone formations. More often than not the sea foamed against dark thumbs of rock offshore. The rough waters littered the beaches with fishermen's nets

and buoys, driftwood, shells, and other beachcomber treasures as well as beer cans and plastic bottles. But whenever the waters ebbed at spring tide, the unfailing show was in the tidepools and rocky littoral.

At first I had overlooked the bryozoans, minute, implausible animals that encrust shells, rock faces, and kelp, but along Cape Arago, southwest of Coos Bay, I learned to identify the yellow, crystalline scabs on the olive blades of seaweed. The encrusting bryozoans, patterned in a lacy weave, are known as sea laces. Others in the group are called moss animals for their mossy appearance. Each patch is a colony of hundreds of animals lodged in separate cases. Stranded on a dry shore, some bryozoans resemble clumps of lacy seaweed, and zoologists at one time classed them as plants.

Each time I scanned the shores and the tidal shallows I saw something new. There were the hermit crabs in borrowed shells, the decorative tube worms holding up bouquets of feathery appendages, and the slow-moving whelks that prey on mussels and barnacles.

Animals of the rocky intertidal do not stray far from home. Even the fishes—the small tidepool sculpins and eel-like blennies—stick close to the same small neighborhood. In sharp contrast salmon make journeys of hundreds, even thousands, of miles before they return to the coast. In summer along the shores as far south as central California, chinook, or king salmon, begin to congregate, awaiting the autumn rains that raise upstream water levels. Coho, or silver salmon, also cruise in coastal waters before entering the rivers to spawn. Scientists have known for some time that salmon rely primarily on the sense of smell to find their way from the river mouth to their ancestral spawning grounds far upstream. Each stretch of the river is thought to have a distinctive odor of dissolved organic materials that make the water smell like home.

"Much is known about the biology of salmon in fresh water," said William G. Pearcy, a biologist at Oregon State University's Marine Science Center in Newport, "but we know little about salmon in the ocean and the early marine period—now thought to be a critical stage in their life history. Juvenile salmon face many dangers during the first few weeks along the coast, when the young are easy prey for seabirds and other predators. One common murre we examined had 13 young coho in its stomach."

In a series of cruises off Washington and Oregon, Pearcy sampled the study area with large purse seines. From the catches in the nets he learned that coho juveniles remain really close to shore, feeding on smaller fishes and crustaceans in cold, fertile waters where upwelling has increased ocean productivity. In 1983 the warming trend known as El Niño raised water temperatures along the shore, contributing to a sharp decline in the coho population south of the Columbia River. As a result coho fishing was curtailed for commercial operators and sportsmen as well.

Other species—lingcod, cabezon, and rockfish—also lure ocean anglers, and during the peak summer months thousands of pleasure boats cross the river bars into coastal waters.

Like many visitors in search of good eating, I took pail and shovel to the sandy shores north of Brookings, Oregon, to dig for razor clams. Stalking this bivalve—shaped somewhat like the handle of an old-fashioned straight razor—was hard work, for its strong foot can pump up and down rapidly, pulling it into the soft sand at the rate of two to three centimeters a second. I took time out to watch the skittering shorebirds. Sanderlings were the most numerous, probing the wet sand with pointed beaks for larvae too small to see. I also paused to gaze at the eerie, flattened shapes of the sea stacks—phantom schooners and galleons at anchor in the morning fog. As it began to burn off, I saw a dark, glistening head pop out of the water without a ripple— a harbor seal or sea lion. Through the thinning fog it gazed for a while in my direction before it disappeared into the abundant world below.

Almost every summer day in northern California also begins with fog, thanks in part to the California Current. The clockwise circulation of Pacific waters drives this current south along the continental edge in a broad, diffuse flow up to 450 miles wide. When the damp air blowing off the current reaches the band of cold, upwelled water right along the coast, the air cools and its moisture condenses. The resulting fog helps the

coast redwoods make it through the parched summer months, explained biologist Stephen Veirs as we halted before a stand of these venerable trees, easily 600 years old, in Redwood National Park. Fog preserves moisture in the trees by reducing the amount of water lost by transpiration through the leaves. We had to bend backward to see the ever-so-straight, fluted trunks taper to spires in the distant canopy of green. Nature's own skyscrapers, the tallest redwoods tower 30 stories above the rhododendrons, ferns, shrubs, and berry bushes that crowd their feet.

The redwood descends from conifers that grew in great forests over the Northern Hemisphere as far back as the age of the dinosaurs. In recent times the species has been confined to a narrow coastal corridor from southern Oregon to central California covering some two million acres. Of this total, about 5 percent remains virgin forest. The national park, which includes three state parks, preserves 106,000 acres of the stately, cinnamon-colored evergreens.

With sufficient moisture and protected from the chain saw, there is little that imperils the mature trees in the park. They resist disease and insects. Even fire does not seriously menace the redwoods, for they have thick bark and lack the flammable resins found in other species.

We stood motionless for a while in the deep stillness of the grove. A thousand years ago, fifty thousand, even a million years ago there were places very much like this. A timeless, changeless scene, it seemed, in contrast to the pulsing shore. But even at the restless water's edge, ever changing amid the ebb and flood of tides, the shifting sands, and the retreating cliffs, plant and animal species have persisted through the eons—defying change.

Filtered sunlight spreads a cathedral glow through Sitka spruces. Salt tolerant, sturdy, and resilient, the species thrives along the storm-ridden coast.

FOLLOWING PAGES: Western sandpipers mass for the April banquet on crustacean-filled mud flats of Grays Harbor, Washington—a yearly event during the migration from Mexico to nest sites in Alaska.

Stark remains of rocky headlands, sea stacks in Olympic National Park, Washington, slowly give way under the irresistible grinding of the surf. Storm-tossed driftwood plays a dual role in shaping the coastal profile. A tool for the ocean's battering assault, the logs help level the shoreline. At rest on the beach, they anchor sand deposits, adding to beach growth and stability of the cliffs.

Tenacious sea palms hold their rocky ground against the churning surf at Bodega Head, California (opposite). In the precarious zone between high and low tides, exposure to air and sun and hammering waves makes life insecure and often temporary; adaptability determines which organisms band the shoreface. Noted for hanging tough, the two-foot-high sea palm endures where other intertidal algae would rip away. Competition for space compounds the stresses; the sea palms, above, anchor their holdfasts amid a colony of California mussels—

which moor themselves with sticky byssal threads (below left). Barnacles secrete a strong glue, cement themselves to a hard surface, then grow shells of limy plates (below right).

FOLLOWING PAGES: *Barnacles extend dark, feathery legs to filter food from tidewaters. At ebb tide the barnacles withdraw into their shells, battening down to preserve moisture and thwart predators.*

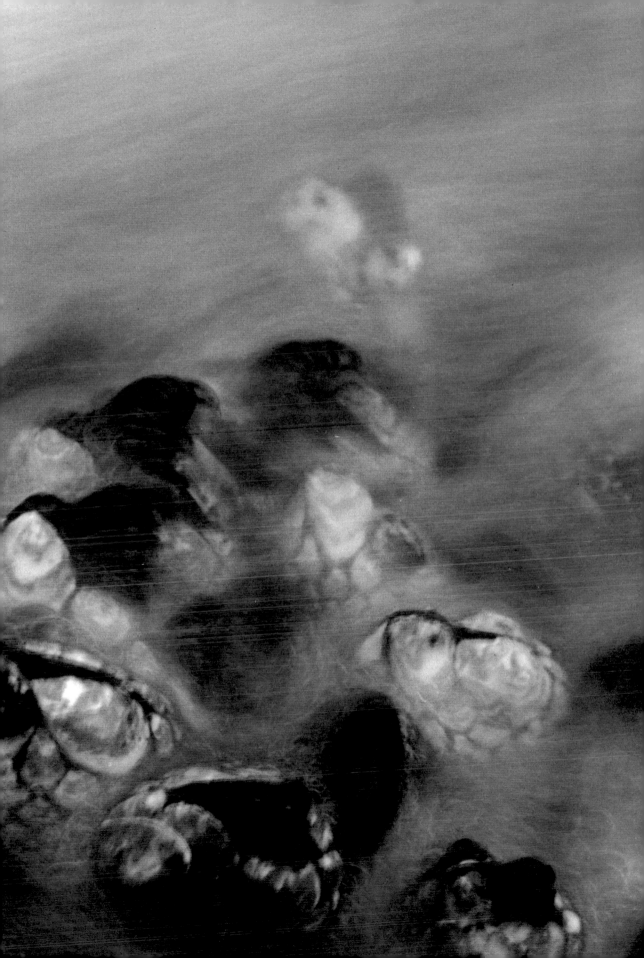

Tiny tube feet of an ochre sea star stretch and strain to get at the meat of a California mussel (opposite). Attached by suckers at their tips, the water-filled feet pull back as muscles contract, forcing the bivalve's shell parts to open. The starfish then everts its stomach—pushing it out through the mouth—to digest the flesh. When the sea star travels, the tube feet stretch out ahead, plant the suckers, and pull the body along. Most sea stars can regenerate severed rays (right); some species regenerate the entire star from a single ray. In a rare display of movement (above), a sea anemone dislodges itself to flee from a leather star. This swimming anemone attempts a getaway by convulsively flexing its cylindrical body; most anemone species stay put, or push slowly about on a sticky bottom disk.

35

Brooding anemones keep their broods close by for the first months of life (above). Born within a parent's body, the young emerge through the mouth and attach to the base of the adult through the juvenile stage. Waving tentacles create gentle currents that move food particles toward the mouth. Familiar residents of the intertidal, flowerlike anemones carpet the lowest reaches of a rocky shore. At Tatoosh Island, Washington, a herd of purple sea urchins (far right) forms a prickly mat around a red urchin, largest urchin species in North America. A phalanx of spines—each set in a ball-and-socket joint (right)—aids in locomotion and defense. When an enemy approaches, long spines react, training toward the threat.

FOLLOWING PAGES: A hermit crab makes itself at home in an empty shell. Crabs grow their own shelter, a hard casing called an exoskeleton. But the hermit has a long, soft abdomen, which it protects by moving into untenanted snail shells—trading outgrown homes for larger models as the need arises.

J. DAVID DENNING. BELOW LEFT: CHARLES KREBS. BELOW RIGHT: TIM THOMPSON. FOLLOWING PAGES: MARTY SNYDERMAN

Undisturbed or overtracked, the gently curved 41 miles of seashore in Oregon Dunes National Recreation Area lend a strange look to the cliff-bound Northwest coast. Sixty million years of earth history—an up-and-down history of tropical seas, mountain building, erosion, advance and retreat of ice sheets—left sloping landforms ideal for dune development. Wind carries the sand and shapes the dunes, some nearly a mile long and more than 500 feet high. Regulations permit off-road vehicles (ORVs) on nearly half the dune area, though they must avoid vegetation. Dune buggies cut new grooves up Spinreel Hill (right), crossing a squiggly web of tracks that document the thrills of careering over the sands. Near Tenmile Creek (above) hikers, campers, and fishermen look out upon a stretch of wind-poured, trackless dunes, accented by tree islands of shore pine. European beach grass, an exotic introduced in 1900 as a dune stabilizer, threatens to cover all the dunes within a century.

FOLLOWING PAGES: Hardy spruces stipple the slopes of Cape Foulweather, Oregon, above the fury of storms like those that engendered the name—and punched holes in the ancient lava base.

THE WINTER BEACH AT POINT REYES NATIONAL SEASHORE, CALIFORNIA; TIM THOMPSON

"We think of rock as a symbol of durability, yet even the hardest rock shatters and wears away when attacked by rain, frost or surf. But a grain of sand is almost indestructible. It is the ultimate product of the work of the waves— the minute, hard core of mineral that remains after years of grinding and polishing."   RACHEL CARSON

The Californias

By Cynthia Russ Ramsay

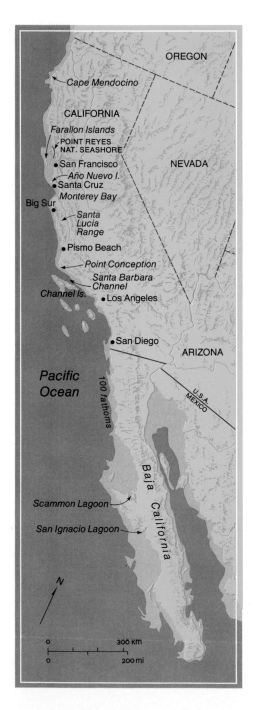

SILENT AS A SHADOW, the great white shark struck. It came from behind without warning, seizing abalone diver Paul Parsons in jaws that held him from his left shoulder to his right hip. With each violent shake of the shark's head the serrate teeth, sharp as razors, sawed deeper into his flesh.

"I didn't see the shark until it grabbed me as I was on my way to the surface," Paul recalled several months after the attack just off Point Reyes in central California. "It all happened so fast, I didn't even notice the pain. My only thought was to try to make it let go." His free right hand still held the abalone iron—the broad blade used to pry the snails from the rocks—and he managed to bring it down on the shark's head once, maybe twice, as he faced those round un-blinking eyes.

Paul was lucky; the lead weights around his waist had protected his vital organs, and immediate first aid kept him from bleeding to death. Otherwise the attack followed a typical pattern in which the 12-foot, 1,000-pound shark ambushes its prey and then suddenly backs away, waiting for the victim to die before consuming it. This strategy lets the shark avoid injury from a thrashing captive fighting for life.

Attacks on humans may be cases of mistaken identity, for sharks do not seem to distinguish between the silhouette of a swimmer or surfer and that of a sea lion or seal—staples of the shark diet. Paul had been free diving, without scuba, in the stretch of ocean from Bodega Head, near Point Reyes, south to Monterey that has become the most active hunting ground of the great

"There is wind in the tree, and the gray ocean's music on the rock." Thus the "sombre magnificence" of the California coast north of Point Conception inspired poet Robinson Jeffers. Below the point the cold California Current continues south, while the coast—the Bight of California—arcs eastward. Here lie islands rich in wildlife, beside terrain rich in oil. And here stretch the golden shores, with the softer music of warm, sandy beaches—still magnificent, no longer somber.

white sharks. Some scientists believe that the sharks may be drawn here by the phenomenal resurgence of marine mammals.

Sea otters and fur seals along this coast had come under pressure early in the last century with the arrival of Russian fur traders. Later, Americans continued the slaughter of sea mammals. Before the era of protection began in the early 1900s there were scarcely a hundred elephant seals along the West Coast; today there are close to 100,000. Similarly, sea lion numbers went from a few thousand in 1900 to 150,000 in 1984. And as the pinnipeds—sea mammals with flippers—repopulated coastal habitats, the white sharks came to dine. Studies around the Farallon Islands indicate that they prefer seals to sea lions and usually attack younger animals.

I would discover many signs of man's depredations and nature's resilience and prodigality as I continued my journey down this prized edge of the continent, where millions make their homes in cities and sprawling tract developments.

Not far from the historic adobe missions, the million-dollar beach houses, and the high-tech industries, the waters nurture the largest kelp forests in North America. Above the surfers and the bikini-clad girls pursuing the idylls of California are skies dark with pelicans pursuing anchovies. Bordered by marinas, orange groves, and fields of artichokes, the Pacific waters provide rockfish, mackerel, salmon, herring, sole, sea urchins, and abalone and other shellfish in hauls that bring in tens of millions of dollars each year. At night during their mating season, so many squid are drawn by fishermen's spotlights to the sea's shining surface that they form a living carpet of white. In the daytime low-flying sooty shearwaters sweep by in flocks of thousands, like swirling clouds of black smoke.

On Año Nuevo Island, a barren chip of land north of Santa Cruz, more than a thousand northern elephant seals haul out, crowding the beaches during the midwinter breeding season. The bulls trumpet night and day as they challenge one another and fight bloody duels for access to harems. Walter Clinton, a graduate researcher in the breeding strategies of elephant seals, described the battling as we boated the half-mile channel to the island, one of 26 reserves established by the University of California to protect natural areas for scientific study.

Despite their bulk—about three tons—the dueling bulls drag themselves across the sand with remarkable speed, Walter told me. In their haste they sometimes trample young pups. Standing chest to chest, heads back, the contestants push and maneuver, seeking to bite the opponent on the neck or on the large, puffy nose that gave the species its name. A tight nose hold often ends the battle, and the sore-nosed loser is chased into the water with a final swipe on the back or hind flippers. The females also display aggressiveness, hissing and grunting and biting as they squabble over space in the crowded rookery. Nursing her own, a cow will fend off a strange pup trying to nuzzle in; but if her own dies or is lost, she will adopt an orphan or even try to steal a pup still with its mother. Unattended, the young yelp and squawk for milk, none more piteously than the orphans.

No such cacophony greeted our arrival on Año Nuevo. The breeding season was months away. The females were at sea, hunting fish and squid. At the landing beach a few juveniles and scarred males lazed in the warm September sun. They were utterly still; occasionally one would raise a flipper and throw cooling sand on its blubbery body. They received us with indolent indifference. A juvenile, blocking our way as we beached, would not move, even when we beat on the sides of the boat. Finally it inched ponderously a short distance and slumped back down.

Northern elephant seals breed at 14 sites along the California and Baja coast. One of them is in the Farallon Islands, which are also home to the greatest concentration of nesting seabirds in the contiguous U.S. To visit the islands—a part of San Francisco, though separated from the Golden Gate by 25 miles of open ocean—I acquired a permit from the U.S. Fish and Wildlife Service, which manages the Farallon refuge. And I boarded the weekly boat of the Oceanic Society's Farallon Patrol, a group of volunteer skippers who transport researchers and supplies to the Point Reyes Bird Observatory Field Station on Southeast Farallon, weather permitting.

As we neared the granite pinnacles and knobs that define the bleak, treeless islands, flocks of pelicans cruised by in long, undulating lines—their broad wings just skimming the troughs and crests of the waves. In the evening the pelicans would return to island roosts, gregarious but silent, since the adults neither call nor sing. Not so the nearly 300,000 seabirds that arrive in the spring to breed.

"Cassin's auklets make a particularly awful racket after dusk, when they return from the open ocean to feed their chicks in the nest," said George Wallace, a volunteer researcher at the field station. "One starts, and pretty soon thousands of them are squealing shrilly. It makes it pretty hard to sleep."

About the size of quail, these chunky gray-and-white seabirds normally lay their eggs in crevices or in burrows dug with their webbed feet. But the auklets also take to the little boxes the observers have set out for them. "It's easier to keep track of the chicks in our condominiums," said George, steering me to a narrow path beside a warren of burrows and boxes. Making their rounds, biologists monitor the chicks' growth and diet. In the safety of darkness the chicks practice flying at the entrance to their burrows. They hop up and down, bouncing like fluffy gray balls—out of sight of the predatory western gulls. These aggressive gulls prey on unguarded young, even pounce on chicks of their own species.

They also swoop down on the eggs of the common murres if the parents don't sit tight. Later in the season the gulls may stalk the fledglings as they jump and tumble from ledge to ledge, making their way down the cliffs to the ocean, where they bob beside their parents.

As many as 45,000 pairs of common murres breed on the island. Not a whole lot, compared to the hundreds of thousands that summered here before the "egg rush" in the 19th century. To feed San Francisco in gold rush days, 400,000 murre eggs were harvested each season from 1849 to 1856. They brought premium prices, and men risked their lives scrambling up and down the treacherous Farallon cliffs to reach the breeding sites and tuck the eggs—up to 200 per trip—into heavy shirts.

In recent years the development of a gillnet fishery has posed a new threat to California's common murres. In 1983, 25,000 seabirds, nearly all murres, along with sea lions, harbor seals, and sea otters, became entangled and drowned in the quarter-mile-long nets. Someone has calculated that 2.5 birds died for every halibut landed.

A dozen bird species breed in the Farallons. Pelagic cormorants nest on the steepest cliff faces; Brandt's cormorants choose flatter areas. Pigeon guillemots seek out rock crevices; the ubiquitous western gulls nest on top of anything, just about anywhere.

Almost due east of the Farallons, on the mainland, the quiet waters of Bolinas Lagoon also teem with birdlife. Sheltered by a spit of land, the lagoon has no waves or strong currents to sweep away the silt and sediment dumped by streams spilling down from Bolinas Ridge. As the tide goes out, leaving only a few pools on the uninviting ooze, shorebirds flock to feed.

"The sandpipers, the small gray-brown birds over there, are pecking at the surface," said Gary Page, director of estuarine and coastal research at the Point Reyes Bird Observatory. Godwits and dowitchers were probing deeper into the mud with long bills. A dowitcher began to jab at the mud, its bill running up and down like the needle of a sewing machine. "Somehow it knows just where to forage," said Gary.

What were they all feeding on? I wondered; the muddy rim looked like a wasteland. "There's more to a mud flat than meets the eye," Gary explained. "The birds have discovered how biologically rich these places are. There are 4,000 shorebirds feeding on what's out there. Incredible densities of worms, tiny clams, insects, and small crustaceans live and multiply in the soft sediments." In one square meter, researchers counted 40,000 small clams; in another, 14,000 tube-dwelling amphipods—crustaceans that can use their legs amphibiously, for swimming and walking or hopping.

Like the birds, the invertebrates also mine the riches of the mud flat in different ways. The ghost shrimp sifts food from sediment and water, excreting indigestible grains in little heaps outside its burrow. The pudgy, pinkish innkeeper worm spreads a mucous net inside its tunnel; the net filters tiny food particles as the worm pumps water through its home with pulsing movements of its body. The innkeeper earns its name by offering room in its U-shaped tunnel to other species, including a clam, two kinds of crabs, and a goby fish. Some take board as well, filching minuscule morsels. It is a life-style science calls commensalism—a group of creatures living together advantageously without harming or benefiting each other.

During my stay at Bolinas I witnessed a rare event. An immense school of anchovies had inundated the lagoon, pushed in perhaps by the tides through the single narrow opening to the sea. They were packed like sardines in a can, so that we could not see the bottom. Pelicans, elegant terns, and Heermann's gulls quickly materialized, and as I looked out across the water thousands of them were massing in tight circles—islands of life gorging endlessly on their extraordinary bonanza.

On the fringes of the lagoon there were patches of green, half water, half land, where hardy seed-bearing plants had created a salt marsh in the brackish mud. The Pacific shore has few sluggish backwaters where these marsh plants take root. Most western rivers tumble to the ocean along precipitous courses, so that the fine-grained sediment is swept directly into the ocean instead of settling down and accumulating to create wetland marshes. Of California's sparse natural legacy of coastal wetlands—a total of about 380,000 acres—less than a fourth remains. The rest was blotted up for agriculture, industry, and urban expansion, or fouled by pollution.

Inside the mile-wide narrows of the Golden Gate sprawls the vast basin of San Francisco Bay. Along its northern and southern reaches wildlife refuges now protect what remains of the marshy shore. In these remnants, not far from the ports, marinas, and hamburger joints, graceful white egrets wade with stiff, deliberate steps, and ducks parade with lines of ducklings.

Fresh water also mingles with the sea at Elkhorn Slough, a 7.5-mile-long tidal embayment on the broad sweep of Monterey Bay. The slough contains one of 15 national sanctuaries established for the preservation and study of estuarine life. The National Oceanic and Atmospheric Administration, which helps fund the federal-state program, describes the intricate process that underlies the great productivity of the wetlands: Diluted salt water, stirred by the tides, mixes minerals and decayed organic matter of the sea with the land's waterborne humus and other necessities of life. The result is an ideal broth for protozoa, bacteria, and diatoms, which nourish planktonic animals and bottom-dwelling filter feeders. These in turn feed fishes, and so on, as the web expands.

I traveled through this protoplasmic ooze with Mark Silberstein, a biologist and program coordinator of the sanctuary. When he shut the outboard off, it seemed as if raindrops were spattering the dark, winding waterway: Anchovies were popping up everywhere I looked. Along the main channel low-growing pickleweed was the predominant plant—as it is over most of the slough. Europeans for a long time have eaten this wide-ranging weed as a vegetable, fresh or pickled. A rich source of soda, pickleweed has also been used in making soap and glass—hence its other name, glasswort.

Looking closely at the jointed, succulent stems, I noticed that many of the plants were red at the tips. That's where the plant stores the excess salt it absorbs from the water, said Mark, adding, "In the winter the tips drop off at the last joint, and the plant is rid of the brine that would interfere with its metabolism."

At times entire patches of pickleweed seem to turn orange, the handiwork of the strange parasite known as salt marsh dodder or love vine. This stringy, orange-hued plant has no chlorophyll and thus cannot make food for itself. Instead it fastens itself to the pickleweed and extracts food from its host.

Among the animals that graze on the plant life is the California sea hare—a relative of snails and slugs, about a foot long, with a bunny-like silhouette, including antennae that resemble rabbit ears. I was told if I poked the squishy creature, it would release a deep purple ink; ancient writers thought the secretion was a venomous witches' brew. (Continued on page 59)

Turbulent seas and steep cliffs collide along the southern edge of Año Nuevo Point; on other, gentler shores thousands of elephant seals haul out for the winter breeding season. Males fight bloody battles (below) for dominance over large harems. At a calmer time of year they bask, ignoring a juvenile in their midst (right). California park authorities offer tours of the bustling rookery each winter.

PRECEDING PAGES: Western gulls patrol the rookeries of Southeast Farallon Island, ever ready to pick off stray chicks. Amid the opportunistic gulls nest 300,000 birds of a dozen species, sharing seasonally abundant food in nearby waters.

ABOVE AND LEFT: FRANK S. BALTHIS. UPPER: TIM THOMPSON. PRECEDING PAGES: KEVIN SCHAFER/HIGH AND WILD PHOTO

BELOW AND RIGHT: THOMAS ROUNTREE. LOWER: TIM THOMPSON

Too much to swallow, a fish stuffs the beak of a baby Caspian tern as elders attend the filling repast in California's Elkhorn Slough. Hoping to fill its beak, a snowy egret stabs at a school of fish in a nearby pond. Freshwater runoff and tidal seawater mix in these Monterey Bay wetlands, producing sustenance for 80 species of fish, 200 kinds of water birds, and, in the mud flats, a notable assortment of invertebrates. One of these, the innkeeper worm, may enjoy a life span of 60 years; its ample burrow offers room—and sometimes board—to fish and crabs. Nine-tenths of the vegetation along the winding channels consists of pickleweed (right); changing color with the seasons, the salt-tolerant succulent tints the slough with green, coral red, and crimson.

Sea hares also feed in the underwater forest of giant kelp, the storied sequoia of the sea that spreads along the coast from Monterey Bay to northern Baja. It grows just beyond the surf, typically in depths of 20 to 60 feet, and anchors itself to the rocky reefs with pencil-thin strands that form the holdfast. The name describes the main function: to hold fast. Unlike a root, the holdfast does not absorb nutrients from the ground.

From the holdfasts extend the fast-growing fronds. A single frond of giant kelp, consisting of a long, ropelike stipe and its flat blades, may grow two feet a day. Buoyed by gas-filled floats, clusters of fronds rise from the bottom like trunks of mighty trees and spread along the surface in dense tangles. This luxuriant canopy dims the sea below. When sunlight strikes the swaying streamers at the surface, they glow like old gold.

"Everything is in constant motion," said James M. Watanabe, a scuba diver and a research biologist at Monterey's lavish new aquarium. "You can glide along at any level and stop anywhere along the whole length of the plant and find fishes and invertebrates all along the way. Schools of blue rockfish hang motionless just below the canopy. Toss anything in and they flash right over to eat it." The rockfish and kelp bass are hunters in the undersea forest. Kelp crabs, turban snails, and shrimplike crustaceans roam inconspicuously among the fronds. Colonies of bryozoans spread a white frosting on the blades. Kelp surf perch hover beside the stipes, fading into the vegetation to elude predators.

The yellow senoritas flit among the other fishes, performing a special service. They pick off parasites in mouths and gills with their pointed little teeth. Sometimes fish will crowd around a senorita, each awaiting its turn at the cleaners. The garibaldi, in brilliant orange hues, is the most conspicuous fish in the forest, cultivating a nest garden on the seafloor. The feisty male clears out most seaweeds and moves sessile animals away from the site; a thick bed of red algae fills the patch, and on it the female lays her eggs.

More than 800 plant and animal species reside in this lush habitat and thus have a vital stake in the health of the kelp forest. When I arrived at Point Loma, near San Diego, the magnificent growth that once blanketed more than three square miles of the surrounding sea was gone. No canopies of giant kelp blotted out the ocean's glare. I saw only a shining emptiness. Severe storms in the winter of 1982-83 had ripped much of the giant kelp from the ocean floor. In the spring and summer of 1983 the residual effects of El Niño raised surface temperatures several degrees, inhibiting kelp growth and causing further mortality. Since then, under cooling water temperatures, the kelp has begun to regenerate.

Giant kelp is harvested on specially built barges under regulation by the state government. It's a multimillion-dollar industry. The algins extracted from the plant make ice cream creamy, improve the texture of frozen foods, emulsify salad dressings, and keep the foamy head on beer. Algin is used in toothpaste, paints, cosmetics, bakery items, and auto polishes.

The kelp itself also sustains the spiny sea urchins. Usually they are content to graze on drift kelp. But during periodic population explosions, or when the supply of drifting seaweed doesn't keep up with demand, hordes of the prickly creatures move across the ocean floor like a plague of locusts on the land, chewing up all the live kelp in their path. The Japanese appetite for urchin roe may change things. In 1984 divers collected more than 35 million urchins with scythes and giant nets for the export market. Within 36 hours after the urchins are harvested off California, the roe is on sale in Japanese markets.

In decades past, preservers of the kelp forests have tried to exterminate the urchins by spreading quicklime or simply by hammering them to death. On one August day in 1971 divers crushed more than half a million sea urchins near

Carmel Bay surf bursts up the bluffs of Point Lobos State Reserve, reaching for the twisted trunks of Monterey cypress and Monterey pine. Defying wind, storm, and spray, trees and sea cliffs compose some of the most spectacular headlands in America.

PRECEDING PAGES: *Spectral silhouettes await nature's onslaughts at Point Lobos. Only two native stands of Monterey cypress survive—this one, and another at Cypress Point near Pebble Beach.*

Los Angeles. Along the central California shore-line from Santa Cruz to Pismo Beach, where sea otters have made a comeback, urchin outbreaks do not occur.

"Sea otters are the urchins' deadliest ene-mies," said Glenn R. Van Blaricom, a wildlife bi-ologist with the U.S. Fish and Wildlife Service. We were on the lookout for these engaging teddy bears of the sea. They often hang out in or near giant kelp, where they find the urchins, abalone, and crabs they like to eat.

Mothers wrap their pups in the fronds while they dive for food; when they're ready to rest or sleep, they'll hold a frond in their paws and roll themselves in the kelp to keep from drifting. Fre-quently several otters raft up and use the same kelp anchorage. Lying on their backs with their heads and paws out of the water, they look like bewhiskered tycoons taking the waters at a spa.

Glenn spotted a pup floating alone just off Monterey's Cannery Row. Then the mother sur-faced, clasping her catch to her chest; the pup charged over to her, squealing for its share. Us-ing her chest as a lunch counter, the mother gave her pup some and ate the rest ravenously. Then she dived for more.

The dining habits of the sea otter may please the kelp cutter, but they infuriate the commercial abalone diver. Both compete for the tasty snail—and both use tools to get it. The hu-man diver pries with an iron called a bottom-bar; the otter pounds the abalone with a rock until it releases its grip on whatever it's clinging to. Har-vesters of other shellfish species also complain of annoying competition from the otter.

Some scientists regard the sea otter as a "keystone" species of the kelp forests, a major in-fluence on the makeup of the kelp community. Urchins and abalones lose out, but they survive, keeping out of harm's way in rock crevices be-yond the reach of the predator.

An adult otter, Glenn told me, consumes food equal to a fourth of its weight each day. The animal needs food energy as well as a luxuriant coat to survive in the cold sea, for it is the only marine mammal without blubber for insulation. Its coat is extraordinary. With 650,000 hairs per square inch, it traps air and insulates so well that the skin underneath stays bone dry.

The lustrous, silky otter pelts, valued in the fur trade, almost led to the demise of the species. California's present population of some 1,400 sea otters descend from a small band that survived along the isolated Big Sur coast. Here the Santa Lucia Range plunges to the sea and creates a sliv-er of shoreline without coves or anchorages. It was virtually cut off from the country until 1939, when the Big Creek Bridge completed the high-way that coils around the cliffs.

Even now much of the region remains a wil-derness. Mountain lions still prowl the semides-ert coastal scrub, gray with California sage; wild boars root around the manzanitas and live oaks; and rattlesnakes lurk in the litter on the forest floor—a lovely intricacy of pink, yellow, and beige madrone leaves.

On coastal bluffs summer drought bakes the grasslands to straw, while the sea piles up against weathered rock and foams onto the pocket beaches of cobbles and sand. A fog bank is a sum-mer presence on the horizon, building up for hours or days until suddenly it sweeps in and swallows the magnificent vistas, and only the soft warbling of the vireos mellows the gloom.

Precipitous slopes and rampant poison oak discourage visitors to the forests, which support exceptional trees: The Coulter pine produces 9-to-14-inch cones. The Santa Lucia fir, a spired tree with long, droopy branches, looks as if it had been designed by Dr. Seuss; it exists nowhere else. In the canyons and washes groves of red-woods ascend high into the sky at the southern limit of their range.

To the south, beyond the hard-packed sands of Pismo Beach, lie Point Arguello and Point Conception, where the coast swings eastward and the cold California Current continues south-ward. Jutting into the sea, the rocky fingers of land block or dissipate northwest winds and heavy seas and mark the beginning of balmy southern California. Here, also, the coast forms the California Bight—a wide-open bay that arcs down to the Mexican border. The ocean floor is slashed by ancient river channels, clefts that beckon divers with beautiful and bizarre soft coral animals—feathery sea pens and fragile, fanlike gorgonians in saffron, rust, and orange.

Oil is the lure in the waters around Point Conception and the Santa Barbara Channel. In centuries past Chumash Indians used tar that abounded on the beaches to waterproof their plank canoes. Today, from the palm-lined promenades of the city of Santa Barbara the horizon bristles with oil rigs.

Just off Coal Oil Point, near the University of California's Santa Barbara campus, 18,000 to 25,000 barrels of petroleum bubble out of fissures in the ocean floor every year. Iridescent slicks shimmer on the surface; a vague acrid odor of tar hovers in the air. Occasionally black goo congeals on the rocks, and soft globules litter the beach. But the kelp remains amazingly clean, for the fronds have a mucous coating that sheds oil.

Surprisingly, studies have shown that animal populations around the seep were larger than those in nearby areas without such flows. "It appears that either the organisms exposed to chronic low-level seeps have adapted to the presence of this crude oil, or that petroleum in low concentrations is not as toxic as once thought," says Robert B. Spies, the marine scientist at Lawrence Livermore National Laboratory who made the discovery. "Right at the source few animals survive except for large densities of microbes that feed on the crude oil. They are the key to the thriving sea life, providing nourishment to the worms, fishes, sea stars, and clams and other creatures flourishing nearby."

These findings do not alter the fact that oil in high concentrations, as in spills, poses a danger to wildlife. No one has forgotten the horrors of the 1969 blowout in Santa Barbara Channel that claimed the lives of thousands of oil-soaked birds. The recent discovery of rich oilfields around Point Arguello may mean more drilling platforms, tanker traffic, and onshore facilities along one of the loveliest shorelines in the West.

The oil industry believes there are also large deposits near the Channel Islands that form the offshore border of the Santa Barbara Channel, and there have been efforts to break the ban on new oil and gas leases in the marine sanctuary that surrounds the islands.

Aloft in a Cessna Skymaster, I looked down upon the Channel Islands National Marine Sanctuary and upon four of the five sere chunks of land that constitute Channel Islands National Park. The fifth, Santa Barbara Island, lay some 30 miles to the south, out of view.

We flew over Anacapa first, then to much larger Santa Cruz, a panorama of gnarled mountains split by a single central valley. Scientists were at work down there exposing the tusk of an imperial mammoth embedded in an old riverbed. For years such mammoth fossils were cited as evidence that the islands were once connected to the mainland, but the theory has recently been challenged. Biogeographer Adrian Wenner and his colleagues at the University of California, Santa Barbara, contend that the scarcity of species argues against a mainland link.

"These are sweepstake islands," asserts Wenner. "Whatever is here likely arrived by sheer chance or was brought over by the Indians. If a land bridge had existed, many more species would have made it out here." The cattle and sheep that have grazed on the islands since the 19th century did not come by chance. They and the settlers who brought them completely altered the vegetation. On San Miguel, sheep nibbled the land so bare that soil just blew away. Not a single tree from the original forests survives.

We flew past privately owned Santa Rosa, flatter than Santa Cruz and given over to undulating grassland. Straight ahead was San Miguel's dirt airstrip, where ranger Tom Cox, the island's only permanent resident, was waiting. With Park Service permission I had come to hike to the great rookery at Point Bennett, where more than 35,000 pinnipeds of six species haul out.

Setting out in scorching sunshine, I found it hard to believe that San Miguel was one of the windiest, foggiest places along the coast. The calm was unusual, for the island lies beyond the wind shadow of Point Conception. "Normally the wind sock is straight out," said Tom. "That means the wind is blowing at 30 knots."

Wind-driven sand helped build the fossil caliche "forests" that are one of the curious features of the island. The sand grains, composed of limy bits of skeletons of countless sea creatures, were blown inland from the beaches and covered the surface of the existing vegetation.

Chemical reactions with the plants cemented the sand and created the calcium carbonate crust, or caliche. The fragile casts remain standing long after the plants inside have rotted away—eerie ghost trees brooding over the barren landscape like crude effigies in mourning.

San Miguel boasts other unusual phenomena. On a rise we encountered the island fox—a small, almost feline creature with pointed ears. It watched us with lively hazel eyes until we came within a few feet; then it trotted nonchalantly away. "On the islands," said Tom, "the foxes have lost a lot of their wariness. There's nothing to chase or harass them out here."

I saw the giant coreopsis only as a withered clump of stringy leaves. In spring the nondescript tangle erupts into a treelike plant with a thick stem up to eight feet high, bearing great bouquets of yellow sunflowers.

We heard the California sea lions long before we saw them. To Tom the distant clamor sounded "like children in a playground." When Point Bennett's beach came into view, we looked down upon a panorama of several thousand pinnipeds. Most numerous and noisy were the California sea lions—the trained "seals" of circus acts. They were also the most active, waddling along on their flippers, wagging their heads with each lumbering step. Several were quite agilely climbing some rock ledges. We couldn't fathom why. More sensible, it seemed, were the two dozen lined up in a long row with flippers in the air to dissipate heat. The northern elephant seals stayed put, plopped on the beach, though occasionally one would hunch along like some gargantuan inchworm.

Point Bennett is one of the great wildlife spectacles of California. Only about half a mile off the shores of the mainland is another: the migration of 18,000 gray whales. From December through February, whale-watchers all along the coast scan the sea for a glimpse of the migrants heading south to the Pacific shallows of Baja, the Gulf of California, and the Channel Islands. Those observers who follow the whales to the desert-rimmed lagoons of Baja witness an intensity of whale activity and gain an intimacy with whales unheard of anywhere else on the globe.

"Every direction you look, you see the whale spouts," said Steven L. Swartz, a biologist who has spent several winters at San Ignacio Lagoon studying these great beasts. The mothers and calves go to the innermost reaches of the lagoons, where for the first month of its life a calf is practically Velcroed to its mother's side, growing rapidly on milk with a fat content that may reach 53 percent.

While a mother and her calf lead a somewhat solitary existence, the bachelors and females without calves romp together in large courtship groups near the mouth of the lagoon. As the amorous giants lunge through the water trailing the vapor of their blows, "they look like freight trains chugging along," said Steve.

He has found them timid but friendly, often allowing people to pet them. He recalled the day a female played rubber duck with his boat: "Every time the skiff drifted into the shallows, the animal would balance the boat on her head, take us for a ride into the deeper water, and resume her play. She did this five times in an hour."

The mothers and young are the last to leave the lagoon for the northward migration. When they have the waters all to themselves, groups of calves and females gather, touching, rubbing, pushing, and rolling over each other in affectionate, exuberant play.

Not long ago the gray whale, hunted for its oil, was an imperiled species. Under international protection it has made a remarkable comeback, its resurgent numbers gracing the lagoons, parading grandly on coastal migrations, sharing in full measure the great feast of riches along the Pacific shore.

Eerie, windswept ghost forest haunts San Miguel, westernmost and most exposed of California's Channel Islands. Calcified sand castings, called caliche, outlast the plants they once encrusted

FOLLOWING PAGES: Sea lions and a lumplike elephant seal loll through the late afternoon light of San Miguel; fog often shrouds the island.

Born of volcanic fires, forged by the sea, Arch Rock forms a symbolic gateway to Channel Islands National Park. Eleven miles from the mainland, the natural bridge marks the eastern edge of the park and of Anacapa, an island of islets (left). Rising sea level after Ice Age melting divided a single super-island into Anacapa and its neighbors to the west: Santa Cruz, Santa Rosa, and San Miguel. While fossils of Ice Age mammals suggest the existence of an ancient land bridge to the mainland, some biogeographers say too few fossil species have been found to support the theory. Few native land mammals inhabit the islands today, but sea mammals and seabirds abound. In 1980 five of the eight islands in the chain, along with surrounding waters vital to the island rookeries, were established as a national park and a national marine sanctuary.

In a submarine forest near Santa Barbara,
streamers of giant kelp sway to the rhythm of the
sea (right). Largest of all kelp, Macrocystis grows
in abundance along the Pacific coast in depths of
20 to 60 feet; it uses the sunlight that invades its
shadowy world and absorbs minerals from the fertile
sea. Unlike a tree, this brown alga has no buried roots;
instead it grips the rock with a tough holdfast (lower
left). Cell walls of the giant kelp contain algin—
the source of important additives for food, cosmetics,
and chemicals. Rapid growth—more than a foot
a day—makes giant kelp a rapidly renewable resource,
allowing multiple annual harvests. The forest also
provides food as well as glades of protection for
a multitude of dependents. The garibaldi hovering
beside gorgonian soft coral, at right, helps protect
its domain, aggressively confronting any that intrude
into its nesting territory. Tube worms and tiny
bryozoans along a frond become food for a kelpfish
(left). Kelp-grazing fishes include some species
that feed on the kelp and others that prefer its
minute inhabitants.

FOLLOWING PAGES: Grape-size floats buoy
blades of giant kelp, keeping them off the seafloor
and thus closer to sunlight. A strong, flexible stem,
or stipe, enables the plant to withstand constant
movement of the sea. Giant kelp may grow to
a length of 200 feet, bending and tangling at the
surface. Harvesters crop the dense canopy without
hurting the growth below.

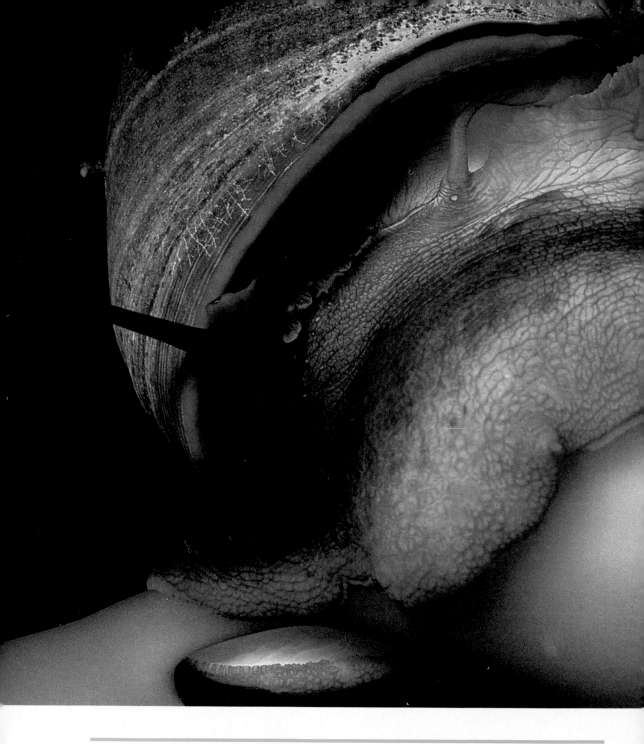

Diverse and colorful, the rich kelp hunting ground harbors more than 800 kinds of plants and animals, from the giant seaweed to microscopic organisms. A top shell snail flares its iridescent body as it crawls over a kelp float (above); by grazing on surface cells, the snail dislodges colonies of bryozoans—the small white patches on the attached frond. A tiny sea star gleans food from other seaweed inhabitants.

Garish hues of a spanish shawl nudibranch (right) may serve as warning coloration to would-be predators. The rows of orange appendages, called cerata, function as gills for the "naked snail," but they also contain stinging cells.

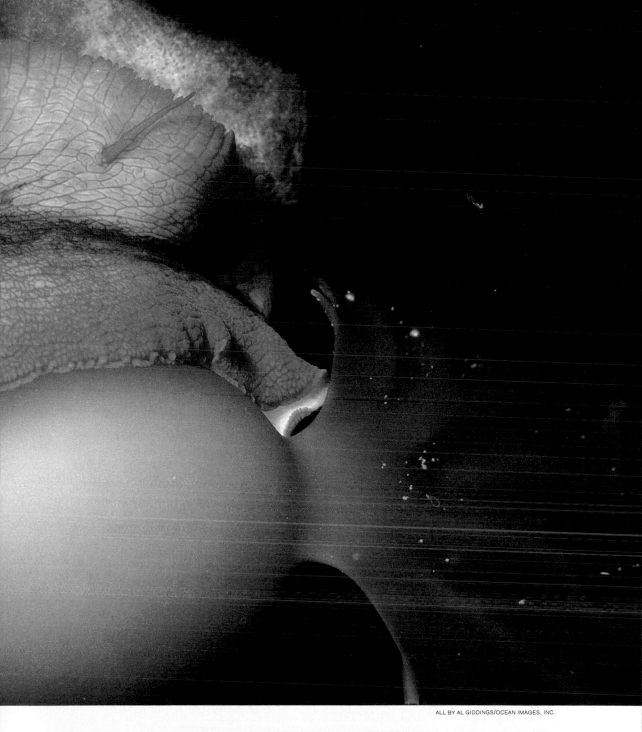

STEPHEN FRINK. ABOVE: BOB EVANS/PETER ARNOLD, INC. ABOVE RIGHT: JEFF FOOTT/BRUCE COLEMAN INC.

For feast or frolic, sea mammals also find the kelp forest inviting. Rafting in a sea of fronds, a California sea otter shucks a clam. Sightseers delight in the scene, but commercial shell fishermen see an insatiable competitor gobbling their bread and butter; the otter eats as much as 15 pounds of sea urchins and mollusks and other shellfish each day.

Streamlined sea lions skim gracefully over beds of southern sea palm near a Channel Islands rookery (left). Off the Santa Barbara coast a gray whale (above left) slurps through the seaweed to strain out crustaceans and other kelp-dwelling animals.

Rolling hills, sheltered beaches, and foamy surf provide inspiration and recreation for artists and writers who make Laguna Beach, California, their home. Formed by sea winds, waves change size, shape, and speed as they interact with the ocean bottom and the shape of the coastline. Long swells from storms south of the Equator end as crashing breakers along the gentle slope of Malibu Beach, making fine sport for surfers (right).

FOLLOWING PAGES: Idling near the surface, its mother never far away, a two-month-old gray whale marks time in the shallow Baja California lagoon where it was born. Soon it will begin its first journey past the beaches, bays, kelp forests, and cliffs of the Pacific edge, to summer in the Arctic.

TIM THOMPSON. ABOVE: FRANK S. BALTHIS. FOLLOWING PAGES: C. ALLAN MORGAN

SUNRISE AT GULF STATE PARK, ALABAMA

"On the sands of the sea's edge, especially where they are broad and bordered
by unbroken lines of wind-built dunes, there is a sense of antiquity. . . . of earth processes that move
with infinite leisure, with all eternity at their disposal."   RACHEL CARSON

Gulf Shores

By Tom Melham   Photographs by Matt Bradley

IT IS NOT A NIGHT for the superstitious: Friday the 13th, hurtling toward midnight, under a full moon that just a few hours ago glowed immense, soft-edged, and blood red. A group of us has spent several evenings on this uninhabited island in the northeastern Gulf of Mexico, searching for sea turtles. So far, our luck has matched the omens of this night. We decide that this will be our last patrol.

Once more the jeep bounces along the shore, past moonlit waves that curl and break, painting the beach in icy phosphorescent froth. Pale armies of ghost crabs materialize, then skitter away at our approach; shadows coalesce and split off from the larger darkness of night. But now one of these shadows seems to stir on its own —flotsam, perhaps? A cast-off tire or plywood slab riding the pulse of this full-moon tide? Or is it merely a shadow, brought to life by our own motion and the trickster moon?

We slow down—yet it keeps moving. On come the headlights, revealing at last our goal: a loggerhead turtle, some 250 pounds of reptilian bulk clawing out of the surf and up the beach to nest. Loggerheads nest only at night, and each landfall is a statement, a stubborn effort of the individual to prolong its species. Just to get here this female has run a gamut of dangers: sharks, shrimp trawls and fishnets, boat propellers, perhaps even some illegal human hunters.

Our armored visitor lumbers no more than 15 or 20 yards from the sea and stops abruptly. At once her rear flippers, alternating like pistons, begin scooping out a hollow. Then they carve a nest cavity perhaps eight inches across and nearly two feet deep, a hole so perfectly round that it seems drilled. The accuracy of the turtle's clumsy-looking but marvelously adept hind limbs becomes all the more remarkable when we realize that she cannot see them; she digs by feel.

Suddenly sand no longer flies; a moment later the first eggs appear, glistening white Ping-Pong balls emerging from the cloaca beneath her tail and dropping into the nest. I am close enough to intercept a few—the flexible, parchmentlike shells are sticky with the female's clear lubricating solution. Within ten minutes six or seven dozen eggs fill the hole. The turtle, which has completely ignored us, now shifts her facile

rear flippers into reverse to backfill the nest. She then trudges back to sea, leaving no sign of her visit except a "crawl"—a yard-wide, treadlike smear of flipper and carapace prints in the sand of this Florida sanctuary.

A month later another turtle leaves the sea about a thousand miles down the western Gulf shore, and again I am there. The circumstances, however, differ dramatically. This one is a ridley—smaller than loggerheads, and the most seriously endangered of sea turtles—and it is just a year or two old. Barely ten inches long, it has come here not out of an urge to nest but because it can hardly function; it is encased in black goo, the result of an oil spill in the Gulf.

These two turtles illustrate the best and worst of the Gulf of Mexico. On the good side, the Gulf is blessed both with great abundance and great diversity of life forms. It may seem flat and repetitive, but in reality it offers a varied continuum of habitats—sand dunes, coral reefs, sea grass beds, hardwood swamps, marshes— each with its ark of animals and plants.

Nor is this biological productivity merely aesthetic. From the waters and adjacent wetlands come about 40 percent of the commercial harvest of fish and shellfish in the United States. The Gulf also means billions of dollars annually in sportfishing, waterfowl hunting, and fur production. Three of North America's four major flyways cross Gulf coastal areas, encouraging hundreds of migratory bird species to stop at least temporarily, and some to overwinter here. The same is true for increasing crowds of migratory humans, who seasonally flock to the beaches and warm waters. And the Gulf provides the United States and Mexico with their number one source of oil and gas. Clearly the Gulf has been both an economic and ecological boon.

But now its incomparable natural wealth seems increasingly threatened. Shrimp harvests vary greatly; oyster beds are disappearing or are often too poisoned for harvesting. Some highly productive marshes are decaying into open bays, while others are turning into housing development ments or toxic waste dumps. Today these seashore wonderlands are at a crossroads.

Unlike the Pacific and Atlantic, the Gulf —by definition—is relatively confined. Its

3,000-mile-long coastline curves back on itself to create a jug-shaped sea whose neck—formed by the Florida Keys and the Yucatan Peninsula—is loosely corked by Cuba. A current from the Caribbean Sea provides the Gulf's heartbeat: The North Equatorial Current enters the Yucatan Channel south of Cuba and exits through the Straits of Florida separating Key West from Havana; thence it flows northward along the East Coast as the Gulf Stream.

Though much of the Gulf shore is ringed by fishing villages, resorts, petrochemical plants, and other development, sizable stretches remain relatively untouched. One is the area around Rio Lagartos (roughly "River of Crocodiles") on Yucatan's north coast, about a hundred miles west of the coral-fringed resort area of Cancun. Although man has hunted the namesake reptiles here nearly to extinction, the land still belongs to nature. Like a winter beach, Rio Lagartos seems somewhat forlorn, besieged by the elements yet strangely peaceful. Even its vegetation

is contradictory. To one side of a shore road rise cattails, tidal grasses, and other salt marsh plants; to the other lies a scene straight from the desert: century plants, prickly pear, Spanish bayonet.

Flamingos—some 12,000 or more—forage in the bays and salt ponds that filigree this coast. They spend most daylight hours in ankle-deep water, heads down, webbed feet gently stirring the bottom while huge beaks filter a meal of tiny algae and animals. At midday they take siestas; from a distance the huddled, top-heavy birds

Diverse shores rim the nearly landlocked Gulf: barrier islands, the swampy catchment of the Mississippi, and mangrove forests in Yucatan and Florida. Oil at times troubles waters that feed migratory wildfowl and nurture valuable seafood stocks. Florida shelters the only crocodiles in the continental United States.

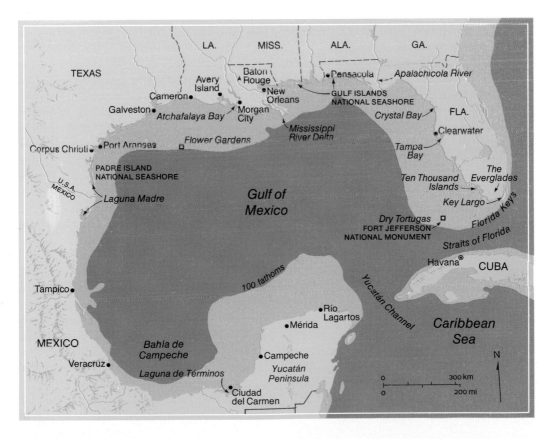

look like so many overgrown pink mushrooms. But approach them and their gawkiness vanishes. They are shy, so dominated by herd instinct that when one flaps up, the three or four nearest it take off as well, prompting their neighbors—and their neighbors' neighbors—to do the same. In geometric progression the entire flock soon is airborne. Legs and necks unwind and stretch out in a flowing line; scarlet-and-black wings beat so silently and slowly that the birds seem mere floaters in time. Effortlessly they scud across the lagoon, a row of fleecy pink clouds mirrored in water. And when the leader alights, the flock again responds geometrically; in a flash the scudding clouds transmute back into mushrooms.

There are also galaxies of fireflies here, making a simple evening drive more like piloting a spaceship through a star field. Millions of tiny points of light swoop out of the blackness, speeding at and past you from all sides. In contrast to *yanqui* fireflies, these do not pulse but remain continuously on. The starry specks race overhead, barely distinguishable from real stars. Here, tonight, an insect's tiny realm and the immensity of the universe have merged—leaving my own world a bit more complete.

West of Rio Lagartos, around the Yucatan Peninsula into Campeche Bay, a 21-mile-long barrier island shields a notch in the shoreline called Laguna de Terminos. The largest coastal lagoon in the southern Gulf, Terminos and its surrounding wetlands fill some 618,000 acres with different ecological crannies. Dense mangrove forests dominate the shore, while shallows harbor vast beds of sea grasses. Three rivers variously dilute the lagoon's salt water, creating different pockets ideal for oyster reefs or freshwater grasses, riverine trees or brackish marshes.

"In the middle of the lagoon and along most shores it's very natural," says John W. Day, Jr., a coastal ecologist at Louisiana State University and a periodic visitor to Terminos. "Pristine? Well, certainly parts of it are. It's more natural than anything its size in the Gulf. There's been no dredging, very little drainage of wetlands. In general the whole lagoon looks good."

Its mangroves grow in seawater, some reaching 80 feet high. Their branching prop roots curve down from as high as 10 or 12 feet up the trunk. They can be as forbidding as any briar patch, these webs of spring-loaded sticks. For though they lack thorns, they snag feet most efficiently, throwing you into leaf-veneered muck. Few human visitors consider hiking through mangroves one of nature's delights.

But mangroves are very important, says Alejandro Yáñez-Arancibia, a professor of coastal ecology at Mexico's National University. The mesh of roots that props up the trees also protects coastal areas from erosion and storm damage. And mangroves harbor all kinds of life. Orchids and snakes hang from the branches, while cicadas buzz and hummingbirds hover; bottlefish, tunicates, and worms dwell in the muddy shallows; the plantlike animals called hydroids and marine snails and other mollusks find food amid the tree's tide-swept roots, where crabs also scavenge.

What fuels this diverse web of life? To a large degree mangroves and their own decay. The trees yield as much as six tons of leaves and other dry matter per acre per year. Add in the organic contributions from all the animals they shelter, says Yáñez-Arancibia, and it's obvious why mangrove forests rank as one of the world's more productive ecosystems. They simply produce a lot of food.

Another productive Terminos habitat lies just offshore in the shallow realm of the sea grasses. Flowering, seed-bearing plants originated many millions of years ago on land, and sea grasses—like sea mammals—descend from ancestors that adapted to a marine environment. These highly evolved plants bloom, cross-pollinate, and fruit while completely submerged in salt water. One of the most successful is turtle grass.

I remember skin-diving in Terminos where silt was elbow-deep and fine as talcum; the slightest motion stirred up clouds of it. All was gray, the color of death. Even the ribbony leaves of turtle grass that blanketed the bottom in foot-tall meadows seemed lifeless and as dusty as a long-abandoned attic. I brushed the silt from a single strand—and found its green surface encrusted with scores of pinhead-size mollusks. Sifting a handful of muck through my fingers yielded spiral-shell gastropods, marine worms, and small black sponges. The more I probed, the more I saw: Inch-long, transparent fingerlings precisely the gray of the silt glided in and out of visibility. Little wonder that John Day assesses sea grass beds "as rich as a jungle."

Like any reservoir of natural riches, however, Terminos faces the risk of exploitation. Ciudad del Carmen, a shrimping and petroleum city of 120,000, clings to the downcurrent end of the lagoon's barrier island. The oil riches of Campeche Bay have drawn so many *petroleros* that Carmen's population nearly tripled in recent years.

Already, oil spills have occurred; but the same currents that keep Terminos relatively free of Carmen's sewage usually protect it from wayward oil. Even the notorious 1979 blowout of Ixtoc I—a platform only 50 miles offshore that bled for nearly ten months—did not blacken the lagoon. Instead, the spillage spread across a thousand miles of Gulf, winding up on beaches from Veracruz to Port Aransas, Texas.

The Texas coast is so oil-prone that some hotels routinely stock rooms with "Tar-Off"—solvent-impregnated towelettes—for guests who venture onto oil-spotted beaches. I was in Galveston in August 1984, just after the British tanker *Alvenus* ruptured its hull in the Fairway Channel near Cameron, Louisiana, with 14.6 million gallons of heavy Venezuelan crude on board. Attempts to contain and collect the oil proved so chaotic that nearly 48 hours passed before any spillage could be pumped up. By then, some three million gallons had escaped and were headed for Galveston's sun-bleached sands.

Waves quickly churned the dense oil even thicker, into what salvors call "chocolate mousse." Day by day this black tide advanced. As long as it kept offshore, too dispersed to enclose with booms or gather up, there was little anyone could do. Dale Hall, field supervisor for the U.S. Fish and Wildlife Service, which administers six wildlife refuges along the northern Texas coast, had weathered spills before. "This is the frustrating part," he moaned. "We have to sit back and wait."

He explained the usual cleanup procedure: Simply let the oil come ashore, collect it with road graders, and haul it away. It's far easier to scrape a few miles of beach than to skim a huge section of Gulf.

Three days after *Alvenus* ran aground, the spillage remained at sea—but an acrid, creosote-like aroma had begun to permeate Galveston's salt air. I was surprised when Hall interpreted this as good news: "It means the oil's weathering—giving off the most toxic materials, the aromatics." On a Galveston beach I found the creosote stench so strong that I looked to see if someone might be tarring a roof. No one was. A beachcombing couple walked up from water's edge.

"Mister, you know what this black stuff is?" the woman asked, her foot spotted with tarry globs. I looked past her and saw black puddles wallowing in the surf. *Alvenus*'s oil had arrived.

I had expected a gigantic sheet of dark ooze coming ashore in one massive assault. What I saw was more a sneak attack: Individual, molasses-thick clumps gradually emerging from the water like slow-motion troops bolstering a beachhead. Offshore, helicopters would sight larger pools of oil trailing jagged black tails. This was the leading edge of a 78-mile-long slick that would leave a tarry "bathtub ring" on Galveston's seawall and pave some of its prized beaches with a 20-yard-wide swath of goo.

There is more to an oil spill than oil-drowned birds and blackened beaches, more also than the staggering costs of cleanup. In addition to being a physical mess, petroleum is a chemical nightmare. Many marine animals have a zero tolerance for it. Wetlands are especially vulnerable, for the wildlife is densely arrayed, and tides here do not flush as fast or as completely as in the open Gulf. Because many wetlands organisms are filter feeders, they readily accumulate the highly toxic oil. Predatory fish further concentrate it, at times to levels that can trigger governmental bans on the consumption of these fish as seafood. Galveston Bay—between 30-mile-long Galveston Island and mainland Texas—harbors miles and miles of productive marshes and estuaries.

Luckily, no oil from *Alvenus* reached Galveston Bay waters. But the wetlands remain threatened; not only *(Continued on page 93)*

Longest barrier island in the U.S., Padre Island
(opposite) curves along the south Texas coast
for 113 miles. Much of it, protected as a national
seashore, wears a natural look, allowing free
interplay of sand and surf; storm surges flood
over low-lying passes into Laguna Madre, and
backrushing waters return to the Gulf. A bit
of cowboy lingo (right) shoos campers from dunes,
to preserve beach grasses—and campers as well.
The man-made configuration (below) brings
seawater moorings to members of the Padre Isles
community north of the national seashore.

FOLLOWING PAGES: Pointing the direction of
prevailing southeasterlies, weathercocked live oaks
filigree a Padre Island sunset.

WHOA PARTNER
STAY OFF DUNES
HELP PROTECT VEGETATION
WHICH PREVENTS SAND
DUNES FROM BLOWING AWAY

CAUTION
RATTLESNAKES ARE COMMON
IN SAND DUNES

WATCH YOUR CHILDREN

Ring levee around an oil-and-gas rig curbs the spread of pollution on Louisiana's Chenier Plain, a prime waterfowl wintering ground dotted by stands of oak, or cheniers. The access road causes less damage to wetlands than would a canal.

Among a variety of causes, including natural ones, canal dredging accounts for a major share of land losses in coastal Louisiana. Maps, opposite, tell a stark tale—153 square miles of marsh and swamp turning to open water in the lower Mississippi Delta.

LOWER MISSISSIPPI DELTA   1956   1978

is the area prone to tanker spills, but it must cope as well with its own oil industry, onshore and off. Also, regional growth has made the wide-open wetlands increasingly attractive as building sites; filling them in puts additional strains on local freshwater supplies and other resources. And even with landfills, the land is sinking.

"Ground subsidence here is amazing," says Dale Hall, "because they're always taking out oil, and water for municipal systems, and never putting anything back." Normally, he explains, groundwater gradually refills drained oil wells and aquifers. But since wetlands, a major repository of groundwater, are disappearing, there is less water to fill the void.

Declining fish harvests—due to wetland depletion as well as overfishing—have prompted government agencies to restock some sport fish species. "What we need is not more fish but more habitat," Hall argues. Provide that, and fish populations will take care of themselves.

One way to protect and even increase habitat is to set it aside as national park, wildlife refuge, or other preserve. Southwest of Galveston, the marshes of Aransas National Wildlife Refuge set a winter table for most of America's surviving whooping cranes. Another example is Padre Island, southernmost end of an island chain that rims the Texas coast. Like Galveston, Padre is a barrier island, long and lean and low-lying, situated just off the mainland and parallel to it. Unlike Galveston, Padre is largely undeveloped. More than half of its 113-mile span lies within Padre Island National Seashore.

The preserve contains beaches, wetlands, and sand dunes; its bay shore defines the eastern edge of Laguna Madre, a super-saline estuary that nurtures vast wetland acreages and provides way stations for incredible numbers of migratory

Spanish moss whiskers the bald cypress above a green carpet of duckweed and water hyacinth in the lower Atchafalaya River Basin. A major floodway for Mississippi overflow, the Atchafalaya receives nourishing silts that build a new delta at its mouth. There, in contrast to the retreating coastline around the lower Mississippi, Louisiana land expands.

birds, including the peregrine falcons that shuttle between the Arctic and South America.

In fact, the island serves as the peregrines' only spring staging area in North America. Hundreds of falcons linger here for several weeks between late March and early May, before continuing on to the northern nesting grounds. It is an extremely important "pit stop," especially for the females, whose bodies must store enough food not only for the long flight ahead but also for the production of the usual clutch of three or four large eggs soon afterward.

Year after year they come to Padre, congregating primarily in a section that seems unlikely for such crag-loving raptors—the sandy tidal flats behind dunes that buttress Gulf beaches. In the words of Scott Ward, a veterinarian who has spent 20 years studying peregrines, these flats "look like the surface of the moon. Endless, totally unvegetated. The first time you go out there, you get scared. You can't see the bay, can't see the Gulf, anything. Just sand."

Heat and high humidity produce a somewhat murky atmosphere, and mirages are common. "You might spot a coyote shimmering along, looking like it's running through a cloud," says Ward. The lack of shelter and the local dearth of plants do not encourage much of a resident wildlife population apart from coyotes, rabbits, snakes, insects, and subsurface creatures. But the location along a major flyway draws enormous migrant populations of chimney swifts and barn swallows, doves and water birds. And so it is that peregrines, hungry for such prey, also come to Padre on their spring break.

Some 100 miles to seaward of Galveston, near the edge of the continental shelf, lie the coral reefs known as the East and West Flower Gardens. Unlike barrier and patch reefs common to shallow waters of Florida and the Caribbean, these are the tops of undersea hills poking up into the blue-water Gulf. Their remoteness has kept them unspoiled, and they recently have been nominated for national marine sanctuary status.

Under the guidance of Thomas J. Bright, a coral reef ecologist at Texas A & M University, I was able to dive the East Flower Garden. Strange to cruise for mile after mile, seeing nothing but the bottomless blue of the offshore Gulf; then in one isolated spot the blue suddenly gives way to giant, umbrella-shaped coral heads. They seem to float, for the seafloor lies far beyond the water's 100-foot visibility.

You drop about 70 feet to the reef's summit, noting its absolute lack of elkhorn and other branching corals, which proliferate in the shallower depths of Florida reefs. Here, huge star and brain corals are predominant, interspersed with plate corals. Some stand eight or ten feet in diameter, each domed head started by a single coral animal that grew into a colony. Almost none, however, remain as a single colony. Star and brain corals grow as slowly as sequoias, adding only a quarter-inch or so to their diameters in a year. Over their many decades, diseases often bare some patches. Other corals quickly colonize the bald spots. Corals may be sedentary animals, but this coral garden is nothing short of a war zone. Each coral head comprises a patchwork where several species have drawn battle lines.

"It's pretty dynamic," Bright told me. "Corals are always growing back and forth, jockeying for space." They also endure the predations of various rock borers and reef browsers, which at times undercut the stony heads, leaving countless shelves and nooks. And these shelter the wealth of marine life for which coral reefs are so renowned. Grazing herds of starshell snails, fluffy feather duster worms, leafy and filamentous algae, crusty-looking hermit crabs, and myriad fish spatter this realm with every color and shape. Large jacks and chubs glide by, barely a yard from my hand, trailed by three or four silver arrows— barracuda! And after them a symbol of the tropics comes into view—a male dolphinfish, some five feet long, its blunt, blue head grading into an iridescent green body that ends in a sparkling yellow tail. It is a gorgeous creature.

The gardens owe their existence to a geological accident known as salt dome formation. About 200 million years ago the evaporation of Jurassic seas left salt deposits throughout what is now the coastal Gulf. Layers of sediment later buried the salt, eventually creating enormous pressures that made it semiliquid. Wherever faults and other weak spots occurred in overlying strata, the salt pushed up, raising the surface into disconnected bumps, today's salt domes. The

Flower Gardens are thin coral caps atop two offshore bumps. Several thousand other salt domes dot the coast and offshore Gulf, but only these two possess all the conditions necessary for coral reefs—sunlight, plenty of plankton, and minimum water temperatures of 70°F.

In Louisiana, locals refer to landlocked salt domes as "islands." Against the flatness of the floodplain these gently sloping structures stand out about as dramatically as a pitcher's mound on a baseball diamond. Perhaps the most famous is Avery Island, home of the McIlhenny Company, which uses Avery Island salt to prepare its Tabasco pepper sauce. But to most Gulf residents salt domes spark visions not of condiments but of cold cash. The domes underlie oil-bearing strata, and as they slowly push upward they tend to concentrate pockets of oil and gas.

Above the Flower Gardens you can see tiny bubbles rising from the coralline surface— evidence of natural gas seeps. The stark profile of Mobil Corporation's platform A-389 only a mile away further affirms the petroleum presence below. Ever since the area was first opened to oil leases in 1974, there has been concern over the Gardens. Usually, oil and corals don't mix, but here they seem to be tolerating each other. While the reef's proposed sanctuary status will not ban oilmen, it will prescribe ways to proceed for everyone's benefit. Living corals, for example, will be protected from damage or drilling— but the industry will be allowed to tap oil reserves adjacent to the Flower Gardens by drilling at a slant from nearby platforms. Drillers must also exercise extra care in disposing of such wastes as drilling mud, a slurry of lubricants and clays used to float cuttings up from a drill hole.

So far, says Bright, the industry has been most cooperative and has even generated some positive influences: The submerged steel skeleton of Mobil A-389 has become a productive artificial reef. In the water only three years, it bristles with thick encrustations of barnacles, algae, and bryozoans, while sea urchins, crabs, blennies, wrasses, and larger predatory fishes also congregate here. Multiply this community by 3,000— the approximate number of rigs in the U.S. waters of the Gulf—and you realize the impact of the industry on the array of life.

94

While coral reefs may boast the greatest biological diversity of any marine environment, observes Bright, the greatest biomass is produced in and near the estuaries. Few people, apart from fishermen and processors, know or care about menhaden, a bony fish harvested for fish oil, fertilizer, vitamin supplements, and cat food. But both in money value and in total catch weight, Bright says, menhaden is the largest single-species fishery in the U.S. And the menhaden depend upon the estuaries as nursery grounds. So do commercial shrimp and blue crabs.

Texas estuaries are hemmed in by a string of barrier islands that leave only seven major passes along the entire coast. These inlets are critical for both larval and adult forms of marine life that normally shuttle between the estuarine nurseries and the open Gulf. For this reason the estuaries have become an environmental battleground. The Houston Ship Channel, Bright points out, is "one of the most polluted bodies of water in the country." Another potential trouble spot: Port Aransas, destined to become the main port for all of south Texas.

"Some of the most productive bay and estuarine environments exist in the Port Aransas area," warns Bright. "It is absolutely certain that there will be a great deal of port development here, and I don't see how it can help but impact the surrounding shallow estuaries."

The threat is not confined to Texas. Shoreline development is booming throughout the Gulf. Bright points to Tampa and Boca Ciega Bays in Florida, where creation of a deepwater port, along with a sharp increase in population and a severe depletion of the wetlands has all but ruined once-prolific estuaries. "That's kind of a disaster," declares Bright.

Then there's Louisiana, site of one of the world's greatest estuaries: the Mississippi Delta, mazed with bayous, hardwood swamps, marshes, and other wetland communities. Louisiana leads the nation in fur and fish production; it is third in petroleum production; it claims 40 percent of the nation's coastal wetlands and more miles of shoreline than any of the 48 contiguous states. Louisiana's abundant shrimp and crawfish, its waterfowl and deer, its plentiful alligator, nutria, and muskrat, its prize bass, red drum, and catfish—all provide evidence for the aptness of its auto tag slogan: "Sportsman's Paradise."

But those in the know ask, how much longer? Pollution and land erosion are rampant. The area also suffers from land subsidence and saltwater flooding. For thousands of years the delta was the fastest-growing landmass in North America; in the past generation it has become the fastest-shrinking. Each year Louisiana loses some 87,000 acres of forested wetlands and some 25,000 acres of coastal marshes. This means an acre lost every four minutes. One recent report provides an actuarial table for four delta counties, or parishes as they are called in Louisiana. At current rates of land loss, the 1981 study noted, Lafourche Parish has a life expectancy of 205 years; St. Bernard, 152 years; Terrebonne, 102 years; and Plaquemines may be gone in 52 years. Little wonder that maps show the toe of boot-shaped Louisiana a skeleton of its former self, drowning in seawater, and all but defenseless against major storms.

Who are the villains? Nature deserves some blame, for sea levels are rising worldwide, and the delta's loose, peaty soil is prone to subsidence. The geological structure of the coast adds to the tendency. But for more than 7,000 years the natural trend toward subsidence has been more than offset by the Mississippi's seasonal floods, which blanketed the delta with the Midwest's richest topsoils. The trouble began when man cleared forests and established farms and plantations, built cities on the floodplain, dredged channels that sped the river's flow, and erected extensive levees and other flood controls. Today the rich sediments are shunted out to the edge of the continental shelf, and the former floodplain is denied its rejuvenating silts. The land continues to subside, uncompensated by siltation. In fact, the rate of subsidence has tripled over the past 40 years.

The worst enemy of Louisiana's wetlands, experts say, has been dredging for navigation and industry. Each time a channel is cut through a marsh, marshland is lost, not only from the actual digging but also from saltwater intrusion. Dredged channels encourage seawater to invade inland, killing marsh plants. The peaty soil, no longer held by roots, quickly succumbs to wave action and storm. The result is a spreading conversion of marshland to open, saltwater bays; as erosion proceeds, more sea intrudes and marshes even farther inland give way.

Allan Ensminger, retired chief of the fur and refuge division of Louisiana's Department of Wildlife and Fisheries, has seen such transformations during 30 years of state service. One cause, he feels, is the man-made Intracoastal Waterway that parallels the coast: "It's probably the most environmentally damaging public works project ever inflicted upon the coastal wetlands—next to the Mississippi River levee system. It intercepts the natural, north-to-south drainage pattern of all these watersheds, and it was put right on the fringe of the freshwater marshes, the prairies, and the cypress-tupelo swamp areas of southern Louisiana."

Numerous other dredging projects have taken their toll. Oil companies have carved access canals through wetlands in order to barge equipment to and from onshore oil wells. A 1983 study by Louisiana State University's Center for Wetland Resources concludes that the canals cut by the oil industry and others, including the Army Corps of Engineers, are the indirect cause of much of the delta's current marsh losses. In place of canals, authorities urge the use of board roads where feasible. Built of boards and shells, the roads are much less damaging to wetlands.

Nor are the marsh losses mere real estate. "You're losing habitat for wildlife," explains David Frugé, a field supervisor for the U.S. Fish and Wildlife Service. "The more marsh we lose, the less carrying capacity we have for waterfowl, furbearers, alligators, just any type of wildlife you can think of that utilizes the coastal zone. We know the main fisheries—the menhaden and shrimp harvests—are at, or very near, the maximum sustainable yields. If you continue to lose marsh, you can anticipate these yields declining. The fishing industry is going to be very hard hit."

In one area around the Mississippi River Gulf Outlet some 250,000 waterfowl found winter haven before dredging operations began. Today, notes Frugé, the total is less than 20,000. Present estimates place North America's waterfowl population at 80 million to 115 million birds, and more of them overwinter in Louisiana wetlands than in any other single habitat. But only as long as those wetlands remain.

The fastest, surest way to reduce damage to Louisiana's marshlands would be to breach the levees. But no one proposes a major uncontrolled diversion of the Mississippi; it would deal a deadly blow to New Orleans and other cities. Yet experts see the need for some controlled diversion of river water—without hazard to the cities—to combat deterioration of the coastal marshes.

"The key," Frugé says, "is to divert water in the upper ends of the estuaries, where you get a trickle-through effect. Nutrients are taken up by marsh plants, and fine-grain sediments deposit on existing marsh. Even though these deposits are in thin bands each year, they will help offset the subsidence problem. Saltwater intrusion will be pushed back." Frugé cautions that such a program cannot hope to equal the Mississippi's natural deltaic process. "I think the best we can hope for is to substantially reduce losses and still maintain a very productive estuarine system."

Evidence supporting Frugé lies just west of the Mississippi channel, in the Atchafalaya River Basin. The Atchafalaya, the largest distributary of the great heartland river, has been maintained as a flood corridor for Mississippi overflow. Although levees rim the Atchafalaya, they sit back from the channel, enclosing a vast overflow swamp. Live oaks drip with Spanish moss. Mullet leap and splash as you boat through watery growths of willow, a colonizer that precedes the oak, ash, tupelo, bitter pecan, and majestic, rugged cypress. It is a twilight realm, alternately drowned and left to dry, home of water moccasin and alligator and wood duck. It has yielded more than 40 million pounds of crawfish in a single year.

At its lower end a new delta is emerging in Atchafalaya Bay; some 15,000 acres of intertidal mud flats, freshwater marshes, and natural levees have emerged in the last dozen years. It has become a major wintering ground for waterfowl. This is the only Louisiana coastal area increasing in size—and it could grow another 38,000 acres in the next half century.

And yet, warns Dave Frugé, the future of the new delta and the river marshes just upstream is not assured. Increasing flood stages in the Atchafalaya floodway system are threatening Morgan City and other developed areas; to protect them the Army Corps of Engineers plans to extend one of the Atchafalaya levees all the way to the Gulf. The effect, Frugé maintains, would be to cut off the spring flow of sediment and fresh water into productive marshes.

Not all Gulf estuaries are as beleaguered as that of the Mississippi. Some 240 miles to the east lies the Apalachicola River, Florida's largest in terms of flow. The river and its tributaries drain some 19,800 square miles of Alabama, Georgia, and Florida; like the Mississippi, it nurtures swamps, forests, oxbow lakes, barrier islands—all interwoven in a dynamic mosaic. Robert J. Livingston, a Florida State University professor who has studied this estuary for more than a dozen years, considers it virtually unpolluted. Nearly 90 percent of Florida's oyster catch comes from the Apalachicola system; so do most shrimp produced in the state's Big Bend area.

In 1979 the lower end of this fertile waterway became a national estuarine sanctuary. Its 193,118 acres make it the nation's largest estuarine sanctuary by far, three times as large as the 14 others combined. The Apalachicola is also an International Biosphere Reserve, sheltering "more rare, threatened, and endangered species than any other place in the Southeast," says manager Woody Miley. "And it's got the largest natural stand of tupelo in the world." Its hardwood swamps and grassy marshes comprise a detrital system that generates nearly 400,000 tons of organic matter each year—and seasonal flooding moves this bounty from floodplain to bay.

If the flooding stopped, Miley emphasizes, the bay would lose much of its productivity. Marine worms and other invertebrates feed directly on the detritus and microscopic organisms, becoming food for shrimp, blue crabs, and fish.

Over the last two decades development has skyrocketed on Florida's Gulf coast, often at the expense of the region's wildlife. The rich assemblage at stake includes the shellfish of the Big Bend region, the manatees that winter in Crystal River, the huge billfish off Clearwater and Tampa Bay, the breathtaking birds of Big Cypress Swamp and the Everglades, and the coral realm strung along the keys.

Key Largo, northernmost of the keys, boasts extensive reef-building corals that draw tens of thousands of divers a year. It also harbors a small but important population of crocodiles.

Not to be confused with its alligator cousin, the American crocodile is distinguished by its tapered snout, greenish-gray color, the presence of two lower teeth fitting outside the upper jaw, and its habitat. Alligators dwell mostly in freshwater environs, while crocodiles are primarily estuarine creatures. They are also more endangered. Only two to three hundred exist in the United States, all of them around Florida Bay, which separates the mainland from the keys.

Paul Moler, crocodile specialist with the Florida Game and Fresh Water Fish Commission, periodically surveys the nesting crocs on Key Largo, and one August I accompanied him. His plan sounded simple: We would canoe shallow estuarine canals, capture all the baby crocodiles we could find, then mark, measure, and release them.

It turned out to be one of my eerier Florida experiences. First of all, I couldn't see. (We had set out in the darkest time of night, since crocodiles are principally nocturnal.) Secondly, the shadowy canals were overgrown with mangroves that continually snagged our canoes. Mother crocodiles prefer these man-made canals—left from development attempts dating back to the 1920s—because their dank levees make excellent nesting sites.

Although we wore miner's lamps, we used them sparingly. Slowly we felt our way through the tangles, accompanied by the occasional wail of a nighthawk or screech owl. Here we were, ensnarled in mangroves, besieged by mosquitoes, and groping through underbrush that—for all I could see—might end in the wide-open maws of some very perturbed mother crocs.

Moler belittled such concerns: "Crocodiles have an undeserved reputation. They're really fairly docile creatures." Adults are scarce in August, at any rate. They disappear soon after the eggs hatch in July or August, and few are seen until the next cycle of mating in February. Hatchlings remain in the food-rich canals, rapidly doubling in size. To find them, Moler scans the water with his headlamp, watching for the bright-orange reflection that indicates a baby crocodile's eye. Once you spot the eyeshine, you silently paddle closer and make a barehanded grab in the water just behind. If you're deft enough, you'll be holding a ten-inch-long baby.

They are surprisingly calm, making no attempt to bite or even struggle. "Just big lizards," Moler smiles. Relatively few reach maturity; habitat reduction undoubtedly plays a role.

Key Largo also includes a national marine sanctuary, as does Looe Key farther down the island chain; both protect lush coral reefs. Some 70 miles west of Key West, Fort Jefferson National Monument takes in the Dry Tortugas, a collection of seven tiny coral islands. Ponce de Leon discovered them in 1513, and named them for the turtles he found there; later visitors added "dry" for the fresh water they found lacking there. The Tortugas offer some of Florida's best scuba diving and deep-sea fishing, in addition to an interesting history lesson. Here stand the remains of Fort Jefferson, nicknamed "Gibraltar of the Gulf" because it overlooks the Straits of Florida, a strategic Gulf entrance.

In 1829 Navy Lt. Josiah Tattnall surveyed these waters and concluded, "A naval force to control the Gulf could desire no better position than Tortugas." Command of the straits, it was thought, would protect Gulf settlements and shipping—although the channel's 90-mile width was well beyond any cannon's range. A natural anchorage just north of Garden Key could serve the largest battleships.

A grand scheme soon evolved. The Army would erect a massive hexagonal fort on Garden Key. This despite the island's tiny size (barely larger than the fort), its lack of fresh water and building materials, its susceptibility to malaria

and yellow fever, and its remoteness. Sixteen million bricks had to be shipped from Pensacola, 500 miles away. Cement and stone would come all the way from New York. An elaborate system of 109 cisterns would collect rainfall for drinking water. Even soil had to be imported for gardens that would help feed a garrison of 1,500.

Construction of the fort began in 1846 and continued for nearly 30 years. It was never finished. Along with the Civil War came rifled cannon—which could breach the eight-foot-thick walls of "impregnable" Fort Jefferson. America's Gibraltar had never fired a shot in wartime—and already it was obsolete. The foundations and walls began to crack as early as the 1860s, and the fort was converted to a military prison.

Today, this remote national monument draws relatively few visitors. Those who come must find their own way here, carry along all their needs, and take out all their trash. It is not a monument strong on conveniences, but experiences. Its richly varied coral communities resemble Caribbean reefs. Its old fort echoes with history, while a surrounding moat shelters baby green turtles—part of a head start program for these increasingly endangered animals. On nearby Bush Key, an estimated 100,000 sooty terns return each March to nest. Both the isolation and the no-frills policy of the monument foster preservation of its habitats.

In light of increasing human pressures, this sort of approach—bolstered with far better foresight than Fort Jefferson's builders possessed—is essential to the future of the Gulf coast and the matchless Florida Keys.

The march of moving sand makes casualties of slash pines on Horn Island, part of Gulf Islands National Seashore in Mississippi. These thin strips of land slowly migrate as currents wash sand from their eastern ends and build it up at their western tips. Trees fall victim to the encroaching sea.

FOLLOWING PAGES: *As Petit Bois Island (upper) migrates, the swelling western end edges into the Pascagoula Ship Channel. Dredging clears it—and the spoil creates a new island off Mississippi.*

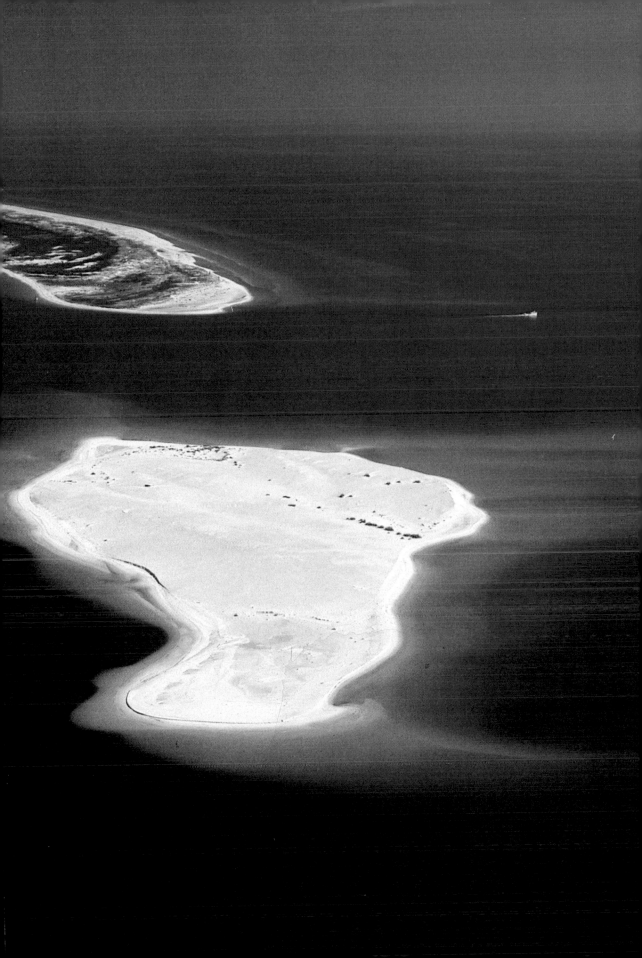

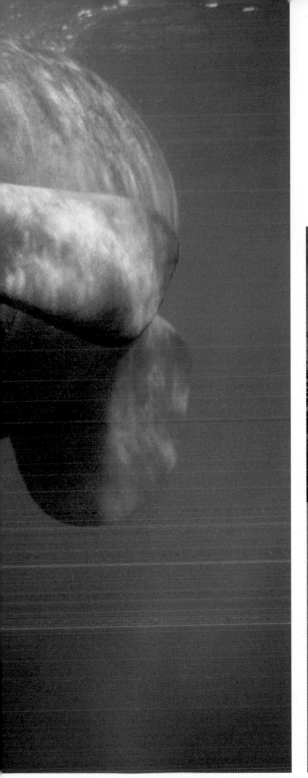

Mammal greets mammal in Florida's Crystal River, where wintering manatees may enjoy company or seek out the privacy of enclaves closed to boats and admiring visitors. Where boats ply the waters, the gentle sea cows, rising to the surface to breathe, risk bloody encounters with boat propellers.

Expander of coastlines, mangroves flourish in salty habitat. A red mangrove (opposite) sprouts amid aerating roots of black mangroves that help the trees breathe. Arcing aerial roots do the same for the red; they also trap debris, stabilizing new land. Ten Thousand Islands (below) create a mangrove mosaic in southwestern Florida. At Big Pine Key a Key deer (above) browses on mangroves, staple of the endangered subspecies.

FOLLOWING PAGES: Sun spotlights an American crocodile in a mangrove swamp of Florida Bay.

Dinner dance of a young reddish egret may reward
the performer in Long Key State Park with a feast of
minnows. Ornithologists wonder if the wing canopy
makes the fishing easier by shading surface glare
or startling the minnows into movement. Human
anglers find great sport along the Florida Keys,
especially on Seven Mile Bridge (opposite), on the
Overseas Highway. The 133-mile road to Key West
traverses Florida's unique string of islands, some of
limestone sediments, some of fossil coral—remnants
of an ancient reef. A few miles seaward spreads the
submerged realm of a living reef, where coral polyps,
secreting lime and aided by plant cells within their
tissues, build colonies of multiform shapes. Here,
wrote Rachel Carson, "living things . . . are able
to turn the substance of the sea into rock."

FOLLOWING PAGES: An ill wind drove this luckless
freighter onto Molasses Reef, inflicting major damage
on living coral in a national marine sanctuary.

Coral kaleidoscope: Queen angelfish (opposite) pokes at a tidbit of sea urchin between sea fan coral and red boring sponges. More than 400 species of fishes roam the coral community, many brilliantly color-coordinated with their surroundings. Famed as an ambush hunter, the green moray eel (below) bides its time between sea fans; the crenellated fire coral in the foreground has a venomous sting. The feather duster (right) filters plankton with its radioles or "feathers"; they retract when danger threatens.

FOLLOWING PAGES: Coral captures a cannon off Fort Jefferson in the Dry Tortugas, where reefs have wrecked ships since the 1600s.

GREAT BLUE HERON STALKS THE EDGE OF THE RUSHES AT BLACKWATER NATIONAL WILDLIFE REFUGE, MARYLAND

*"Here are wide, silent spaces where the wind blows over seas of marsh grass and the only living things
are the birds and the small, unseen inhabitants of the marshes."*   RACHEL CARSON

The Southeast

By Suzanne Venino   Photographs by Stephen J. Krasemann

ON SATURDAY, SEPTEMBER 8, the National Hurricane Center reported a tropical storm off the east coast of Florida. Over the next day the swirling mass of air picked up speed as it rotated around a central core. By Monday morning, with winds exceeding 74 miles an hour, tropical storm Diana had accelerated into hurricane status—the first hurricane of 1984.

Sucking energy from the warm waters of the Gulf Stream, Diana churned wildly as she moved northeast. With only a slight change in direction, the storm would batter a heavily populated coastline. Residents of the endangered area were urged to head for higher ground, and the National Guard was called out to assist the evacuation. Military aircraft were flown inland. Navy ships set out to sea; open water was safer than a concrete pier. News updates classified the storm as "dangerous," "the most powerful hurricane of the century," "a killer." By Tuesday night Diana's 135-mile-an-hour winds hovered off Wilmington, North Carolina, as people waited nervously to see which way she'd go.

The worst threat was the flooding that accompanies a storm surge, a dome of water formed around the low-pressure eye of the hurricane. Forecasters predicted a devastating surge of up to 12 feet. If it hit at high tide, the destruction would be even greater.

Spinning toward land, Diana struck Thursday morning. She ripped up roofs and snapped power lines. Torrential rains smashed windows. At Carolina Beach, one of the hardest hit areas, the water tower toppled like a Tinkertoy, boats sank at their moorings, and a condominium under construction collapsed into rubble.

And yet Carolina Beach was lucky. Diana had lost much of her force at sea, and she hit at low tide. The feared storm surge never materialized. When Hurricane Hazel rammed this area in 1954, a 17-foot storm surge swept away 352 of 357 houses in the nearby town of Long Beach. And as Hazel pummeled the shore from South Carolina to New York, she left 95 dead. Three deaths were attributed to Diana. In the fall of 1985 Hurricane Gloria came blustering up from the tropics, heralded—like Diana—as the storm of the century. Once more the coast battened down. But, again like Diana, Gloria delivered less than she threatened—though damage was severe and 16 storm-related deaths were reported.

Because of their range and power, hurricanes can be the most devastating of all storms. Brewing in the tropics during summer and fall, a hurricane begins as a low pressure area rotating counterclockwise over the ocean. Heat speeds up the spin. As the whirlwind grows, it moves westward, often tracking along the warm-water current in the Caribbean, the Gulf of Mexico, or the Atlantic—where the Gulf Stream parallels much of the coast. The Stream moves along the edge of the continental shelf, 3 to 90 miles offshore, flowing like a great river within the sea. Its warmth affects East Coast temperatures all the way to Cape Cod.

I traveled this region from the subtropic shores of Florida's Biscayne Bay to the temperate waters of Chesapeake Bay. It is a landscape of subtle beauty, of quiet marshes, open bays, barrier islands, and wide sand beaches. Day to day, little change is seen. The drama of this seacoast is weather. Hurricanes passing offshore and winter storms regularly remodel the shoreline. Less frequently a hurricane strikes the coast directly, opening or closing inlets and washing away large chunks of beach. In less than a day Diana stripped away some 20 to 30 feet of beachfront.

"Natural beaches survive storms without any problem," Orrin Pilkey, professor of geology at Duke University, told me after we had viewed the aftermath of Diana. "The coast protects itself with beaches and dunes. Sand dunes help to dissipate wave energy. They also act as reservoirs of sand. Storm waves remove sand from the beaches and deposit it offshore in ridges and bars. Most of the sand will come back as fair weather waves simply push it back up the shoreface."

Sand cushions the coast from the ravages of the sea. It is a function the beach performs well, at least until something is put in its way. During the booming 1920s developers went to work on the southernmost of the sandy barrier islands along this coast. Buildings rose on flattened dunes, and Miami Beach, warming northerners with its subtropical winters, grew into one of the most densely populated resort areas in the world.

"Miami Beach is a perfect example of how *not* to develop the beachfront," said Pilkey.

"They built right out on the sand, out to the mid-tide line. Miami Beach lost half of its beach to construction. We've coined a word for this type of development. We call it 'Floridazation.' To be fair though, Miami Beach was developed before people were aware of the long-range effects of such construction."

By the 1950s the long-range effects were obvious. Without the vital sand dunes, most of the remaining beach had eroded away. At high tide waves lapped against beachfront buildings. There were wisecracks about Miami Beachless.

In 1977, after more than 20 years of planning, a massive restoration was under way, combining the efforts of the county, state, and federal governments. "We studied such factors as wave height, slope of the beach, and the size of sand particles," said Ed Swakon, who helped plan the project for the county. Imported sand couldn't be too fine or too coarse or it wouldn't respond well to the existing wave climate—the height and frequency of the waves.

It took five years and 14.2 million cubic yards of sand dredged from offshore sites—and Dade County had 300 feet of brand-new beach. "Now there's enough sand out there to act more like a natural system," said Ed. "Hopefully, when the next big hurricane strikes, the beach will keep property damage from wave attack and flooding to a minimum."

Block after block of high-rise hotels and apartments walled off the ocean view as I drove through a corridor of Miami Beach. In the low sun of late afternoon, sunbathers here find themselves literally in the shadow of development.

Wind, wave, and weather shape—and reshape—the sandy southern shores, keeping the beaches of barrier islands ever on the move. Behind the barriers, where salt water mixes with fresh, lie fertile marshlands, vital habitat for marine life and for flocks of waterfowl that come and go in their seasons. Intensive development jars the natural rhythm of the coastal zone, from shorefront resorts with disappearing beaches to capacious Chesapeake Bay and its hard-pressed estuarine nurseries.

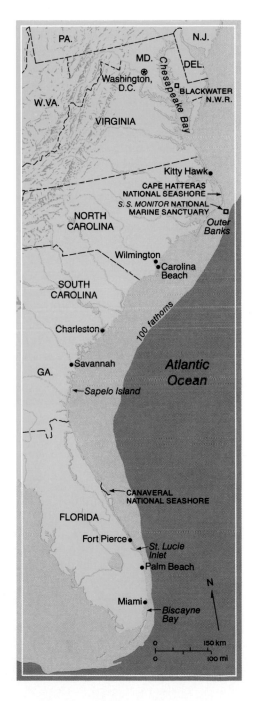

Across Biscayne Bay, the mainland city of Miami expands steadily skyward.

Metropolitan Miami anchors the northern end of Biscayne Bay. As the area grew, the strains of urbanization greatly reduced the bay's water quality. The environment was further altered as the mangrove wetlands were destroyed and the bay bottom was dredged and filled to construct causeways and man-made islands. The clean-up efforts of recent years have been successful in northern Biscayne Bay; and the mangrove shores, coral keys, and clear turquoise waters of the southern bay are protected in Biscayne National Park.

As I drove coastal highway A1A through Florida, I noticed construction cranes perched above the beaches like birds on a fishing pier. Everyone, it seems, wants to live by the sea or at least vacation there. But at Canaveral National Seashore I discovered 24 miles of natural beach, the longest stretch of undeveloped Atlantic coast in Florida. Here, a single 15-foot-high dune runs the entire length of the preserve. With flexible stalks that yield to the wind, slender sea oats fringe the dune crests. This tall, perennial grass helps to build and stabilize the dunes. Windborne sand drops as it hits the grass. Then, as the dune rises, the plant sends out new shoots that bind the sand in place; the extensive root system grows deeper to find moisture. Though sea oats need some fresh water, they easily absorb water from salt spray and even gain nutrients from it.

Salt spray, sandy soil, wind, heat, and scant fresh water create a harsh environment for plants and animals. In fact very few animals are visible on the beach. Most burrow into the moist sand. Consider, for example, the mole crab. This egg-shaped digger migrates with the tides, making its home in the swash zone, the area where dying waves send a thin layer of water up the beach.

When a wave rolls in, explained biologist Ken Leber, the mole crab jumps out of the sand and is washed up the beach with the wave. Then it quickly digs into the sand. As the wave flows back over the mole crab, it traps plankton in its feathery antennae and drags the antennae through its mouth to feed.

"The beach may look barren," continued Leber, who is with the Harbor Branch Foundation, a research laboratory in Fort Pierce, "but an amazing number of animals live right in the swash zone—mole crabs, coquina clams, and many kinds of worms. Microscopic animals live between individual grains of sand. All these attract more animals. A pompano, for example, will swim right up into an inch of water, flopping on its side, to snap up coquinas and mole crabs. At night, ghost crabs often leave their burrows on the upper beach to feed in the swash zone."

The most obvious animals on the beach are the shorebirds. Wandering along the national seashore, I saw tiny sanderlings dart ahead of waves like children playing tag with the water. Sandpipers and gulls foraged among clumps of *Sargassum* that littered the high tide line.

This storied seaweed, a brown alga, grows in shore lagoons and also on the ocean's surface in the Sargasso Sea, a giant, stagnant eddy in the center of the North Atlantic measuring some 3,000 by 1,350 miles. Columbus encountered it on his voyage of discovery in 1492. The dense carpet of weed alarmed his sailors, and there were murmurings against the admiral. The caravels sailed through, but the aura lived on; mariners shunned the sea for long centuries out of fear of being trapped in the tangle. From the edges of the Sargasso Sea the *Sargassum*, also called gulfweed, drifts into the Gulf Stream and some eventually washes ashore.

On occasion large rafts of gulfweed and sea grasses have shut down power plants that use ocean water for cooling their condensers.

In September 1984 the St. Lucie nuclear power plant on Hutchinson Island, Florida, shut down for 11 days with a clogged intake. This time it wasn't seaweed, but a swarm of jellyfish extending some 50 miles along the coast.

Scientists do not fully understand what causes such large congregations, said Peter Anderson, an expert on jellyfish at the University of Florida. Wind and current play a large role in their distribution; food supply is also important. This vast swarm could have come out of the Gulf Stream. The current meanders widely, Anderson noted, and the meanders often form eddies that spin off as gyres, or spirals. If one of these contained a mass of jellyfish, they too would spin off, carried along with the drift of the gyre.

Leaving Florida and heading north, I entered a different world, one that repeatedly inspired Georgia's 19th-century poet laureate, Sidney Lanier: "Look how the grace of the sea doth go / About and about through the intricate channels that flow / Here and there, / Everywhere, / Till his waters have flooded the uttermost creeks and the low-lying lanes, / And the marsh is meshed with a million veins."

Georgia's salt marshes—which include the marshes of Glynn rhapsodized by Lanier—are the most extensive on the eastern seaboard, great prairies of *Spartina alterniflora,* or smooth cordgrass, flourishing in the intertidal zone between the mainland and the barrier islands. And since, like the poet, I would I could know what swimmeth below, I journeyed to Sapelo Island, where the University of Georgia Marine Institute studies salt marsh ecology.

As the ferry to Sapelo eased away from the dock, two porpoises appeared at the bow, diving and surfacing in unison as they escorted the boat through Doboy Sound. Terns dipped and wheeled overhead. Nearly ten miles of *Spartina* marsh separates Sapelo from the mainland and for the half-hour boat ride my vision of the world was the vivid blue of sea and sky and endless fields of shimmering green.

"*Spartina* thrives here because it can withstand high salinity," said Steve Newell, one of the resident scientists, as we tramped through chest-high cordgrass. "Twice a day the incoming tides flood the marshes. *Spartina* takes in seawater through its roots and then exudes the salt through leaf glands." He held up a blade to show me flecks of salt crystals sparkling in the sunlight.

Steve and I were exploring the marsh at low tide, and the muddy bottom lay exposed. Watching the ground as I walked was dizzying, for there was movement everywhere as fiddler crabs scurried out of our path. About an inch in length, they are called fiddlers because the male has an oversize claw that resembles a fiddle. It's always waving this way and that and seems to be used for signaling, defense, and in courtship ritual. Scientists estimate that as many as a million fiddler crabs inhabit an acre of marsh.

"At low tide fiddlers come out of their burrows to feed on algae, bacteria, and microscopic animals that they detect chemically in the mud," Steve told me. With a stereophonic sound like millions of little lips smacking, the crabs busily shoveled mud into their mouths, sieved out the food, and discarded the rest in miniature mudballs on the marsh floor.

Mussels and oysters poked out of the mud. Filter feeders, they open their hinged shells to strain plankton from water that washes over them. Legions of periwinkle snails clung to stalks of cordgrass, gleaning microorganisms from the leaf surfaces. When the water rises, periwinkles crawl to the leaf tops to escape predators that swim in with the tide. Fiddler crabs retreat to the safety of their burrows.

"At high tide you can see the tails of red drum sticking out of the water as they suck fiddlers out of their burrows," said Steve. "Yesterday I went fishing and caught a three-pound red drum. When I cleaned it there were about 150 fiddler crabs in its stomach."

We walked back to the island along a raccoon trail, one of a network of narrow paths worn bare of vegetation by coons that arrive nightly to feed in the marsh. A clapper rail squawked and katydids buzzed in the trees. Herons and egrets waded in the shallows, silently stalking fish.

"What's fascinating about the marsh is that most of what happens here you can't see." Steve explained. "Like an iceberg with its massive bulk concealed, the salt marsh is an ecosystem containing many, many levels of microscopic life. For instance, considering the acres and acres of cordgrass, there are very few dead leaves on the marsh surface, and we wondered why. Well, we discovered that as soon as a leaf falls it is quickly shredded and consumed by microscopic animals and bacteria. This rich detritus soup then becomes food for other marsh life."

An enormously productive ecosystem, the salt marsh yields about 18 tons of grass, leaves, and stems per (*Continued on page 127*)

Waves on a slant gnaw at the sands of Miami Beach, southernmost of the sand-beach barrier islands on the Atlantic coast. In the lee of the barrier, sailboats skim the quieter waters of Biscayne Bay (below), bordered by the towers of the mainland city of Miami. The wave pattern at the beach sweeps sand southward—away from the tanning grounds of the high-rise hotels. In addition, say geologists, a rise of about one foot per century in the sea level gradually pushes the barrier islands shoreward. Florida's popular resort, left with only a sliver of sand in front of luxury hotels, replaced its beach with sand dredged offshore. Technology saved the day, but only temporarily; experts foresee the need for replenishment every five to seven years. A major hurricane could wash away the beach in a day. At scores of sites, coastal engineering fights the battle against shifting sand, to keep it where it's wanted—or to keep it away. Up the Florida coast, at Lake Worth Inlet, a pumping plant shunts drift sand across the passage through a pipeline, to reduce shoaling at the entrance to the port of Palm Beach.

ABOVE: MATT BRADLEY

White sand beaches rise to vegetated dunes on Sapelo, an undeveloped barrier island in Georgia. Subjected to heat, drought, salt spray, and blowing sand, only highly specialized plants survive here. Thick, waxy leaves of Spanish bayonet (foreground) protect against rapid water loss. Sand piling around sea oats (left) stimulates top growth and also extensive root growth downward and outward, helping to build and stabilize the dune. Sprouting from seeds brought by storm waves, beach morning glory (far left) blooms along the high tide line.

acre per year. It has long been thought that marsh nutrients were washed out to sea by the tides. But new research, Steve told me, suggests that most grass nutrients stay in the marsh until animals that feed on them, directly or indirectly, migrate out.

The white shrimp, that tasty crustacean most commonly seen on a bed of lettuce with dollops of cocktail sauce, is a good example. A female shrimp spawns in deep waters, releasing a million or more eggs. After the eggs hatch, the larvae make their way into the salt marsh. Here, protected in the estuary, the larvae feed on microscopic invertebrates, grow rapidly into adulthood, and migrate back to sea.

From the beach of Sapelo I watched fleets of shrimp boats trawling the offshore waters. Their nets scooped up an incredible menagerie of sea life. Over the years the contents of those nets have worried conservationists. The southeastern shrimping industry, according to the National Marine Fisheries Service, inadvertently hauls up some 45,000 sea turtles, most of them loggerheads, each year. About a quarter of those turtles do not survive. With help from shrimpers the fisheries service devised an oval cage with baffles that force the turtles out of the net through a trapdoor. Conservationists are enthusiastically promoting the "turtle excluder."

As the fishermen off Sapelo sorted out the shrimp and edible fishes and tossed everything else overboard, raucous gulls, terns, and brown pelicans trailed the boats to scavenge the culls.

I, too, scavenged as I wandered the shore, searching for seaside souvenirs that now adorn my office and home. At first I discarded all but the most perfect shells. Later I began to appreciate the bits and pieces, the small architectural

---

Surrounded by air it cannot breathe, a ghost crab scuttles down to the sea to wet its gills. This sand-colored crustacean inhabits the upper beach, burrowing down to escape the day's heat and extracting oxygen from seawater it carries in a gill chamber. At night swarms of ghost crabs emerge from their burrows to hunt mole crabs and sand fleas or scavenge debris from the strandline.

details: the simple whorl of a channeled whelk, or the elegant spiral pattern of a moon snail. The architecture of shells so impressed the modern master Frank Lloyd Wright that he used them as exemplars to his students. In shells, he wrote, we see "a housing with exactly what we lack—inspired form. . . . The beauty of their variations is never finished."

I picked up fragments of clam shells for their delicate pinks and deep purples, and pocketed cockles so scoured by time and the elements that their fluted ridges were but a faintly etched memory. Many shells had tiny holes in them. I learned that this was the work of the moon snail.

A gastropod—meaning that it has a foot extending from its stomach—the moon snail uses its huge foot for locomotion as it plows along until it finds a whelk, clam, or even another moon snail. Grasping its prey with its foot, the snail softens the shell with an acid and then drills into it with a file-like tongue called a radula. The moon snail scrapes out the flesh and eats it, leaving an empty shell with a perfectly round hole.

Fascinating, these creatures of the sea, many of them little changed through the ages. Horseshoe crabs have inhabited the seas for more than 360 million years. Not actually crabs, but marine spiders that evolved hard shells, these living fossils come ashore in huge numbers each spring to mate on the barrier beaches.

Compared to horseshoe crabs, the barrier islands are one of nature's more recent creations. According to one theory, the islands are the tops of former dunes—isolated from the mainland as melting Ice Age glaciers brought a rise in sea level. There are other theories, but whatever geologic forces molded these restless pieces of real estate, the basic mix of beach, forest, and marsh was the consistent result.

In Georgia, wide beaches with high, vegetated dunes front dense maritime forests of pine, bay, and palmetto. Live oaks, some of them hundreds of years old, grow in strange, contorted shapes, their limbs draped with veils of Spanish moss and tangles of grapevine. Most of the Georgia barrier isles, also called sea islands, were antebellum plantations; many were postbellum resorts of wealthy northerners. Yet today most are undeveloped, preserved by environmentally conscious individuals or institutions. The islands cast a haunting, primeval spell.

A flight along the South Carolina coast told a different story. Here I viewed a seaside corridor of condos, cottages, and luxury homes. Many sat dangerously close to the water and with the next big storm—or the one after that—some of them would surely be hit. Winter storms, I was told, claim one or two houses a year. The beaches were girded with seawalls and groins in futile attempts to halt the movement of the shore.

"A war has erupted at the American shoreline," writes geologist Orrin Pilkey. "One of the belligerents is a rising sea level. . . . Facing this formidable enemy are thousands of well-to-do Americans who want to live right on the seashore." As the sea level rises, America's barrier islands are retreating—at an average rate of two or three feet a year, Pilkey estimates. And as beaches erode, sea and storm engage the costly defenses deployed to shore up valuable shorefront investments.

Island dwellers of earlier times tried to live with the shifting sands. They built away from the shorefront, on the safer, forested side of an island; or they built on long, narrow lots so that houses could be moved as the ocean came closer.

In most instances where man tries to mold the coastline to his will, man is the loser. Yet here in South Carolina I discovered a unique example of man working hand in hand with nature—by judicious dumping on the ocean bottom. "Some people might think we're in the scrap metal business, I won't deny it," said Mel Bell, director of South Carolina's artificial reef program. "But what's so remarkable about artificial reefs is that they work so easily and so well. After we've done our part, which is simply to place the suitable material in a carefully selected site, nature does the rest."

You can start with an old school bus, cars, rubber tires, or concrete rubble. "Our reefs are made predominantly of boats, barges, and landing craft," said Mel as we motored toward Capers Reef, some 12 miles out of Charleston Harbor. "Instead of scrapping the vessels, shipyards and other companies donate them to us. The first thing we do is make sure they're environmentally safe. We make sure all the fuel tanks have been

pumped and that there are no other residual hydrocarbons left. We remove all floatable objects and strip down any masts or stacks so they usually stand no higher than 20 feet off the bottom. Then we tow it out to sea and sink it, either by opening the valves to flood it or by using explosives." Marine organisms quickly colonize the structures, and a bit of empty seafloor is transformed into a thriving reef community.

Mel and I donned scuba gear and rolled over the side of the boat. We were going diving on a steel-hulled fishing trawler sunk just nine months earlier. Descending along the anchor line to a depth of 45 feet, I could see a large shadow looming ahead. As I swam closer, the outline of a boat came into focus. Black sea bass, white bone porgies, and sheepshead circled. Schools of spadefish ambled by. Silvery grunts flashed, turning smartly in formation. Huge amberjack, about four feet long, swam within inches of me. A lone barracuda watched the passing parade. Barnacles and algae encrusted the trawler. A tiny blenny peered out of a crevice with eyes that seemed enormous for its two-inch length.

"The Japanese first used artificial reefs about 200 years ago," said Mel, back on the boat. "They have developed the technology to the point where they are now engineering concrete, steel, and fiberglass structures specifically as artificial reefs and have used them to build multimillion-dollar commercial fisheries."

South Carolina's 16 man-made reefs are used for recreational fishing. The Wildlife and Marine Resources Department publishes the location of each and also of six shipwrecks that the state monitors for the same purpose. "The old wrecks," said Mel, "are so overgrown they look like natural reefs. You can hardly tell you're looking at a ship."

Hundreds of wrecks lie scattered in the turbulent waters and shifting sandbars of Diamond Shoals off North Carolina's Outer Banks, a narrow string of barrier islands elbowing out into the Atlantic, with Cape Hatteras at the crook.

Near the cape the Gulf Stream sweeps close to land. For centuries these waters served as important sea lanes for sailing ships traveling north with the favoring Gulf Stream or south with the Virginia Coastal Drift, a finger of the cold-water

Labrador Current. Many a voyage ended here as storm and shoal took their toll.

In this graveyard, 16 miles southeast of Cape Hatteras, lies the historic ironclad *Monitor*, America's first gunboat with a revolving turret. Early in 1862 her inconclusive duel with the Confederate ironclad *Merrimack* had sounded the death knell of wooden warships. Then, on the last day of that year, en route to join in an assault on Wilmington, North Carolina, *Monitor* met her match: a Hatteras gale that sent her to the bottom. It was not until 1973 that searchers pinpointed the grave; a century had turned the famed "cheesebox on a raft" into a thickly barnacled artificial reef. In 1975 this historical and archaeological treasure was established as the nation's first national marine sanctuary—a status that assures some protection but cannot thwart the corrosive sea, which slowly eats away at the old skeleton.

During the *Monitor*'s fatal voyage seamen from an accompanying ship took navigational fixes on the lighthouse that had been signaling from Cape Hatteras since 1803. In that year the lighthouse keeper recorded more than a mile of beach out front. When a taller lighthouse replaced the original one in 1870, about 1,500 feet remained. Today, at high tide in winter, the beach may measure only 150 feet.

Over the years a number of techniques have been employed in efforts to fend off the sea. I looked down upon some of them as I stood on the observation deck of the 208-foot structure, tallest brick lighthouse in the nation. Steel and concrete groins extended into the ocean. Large nylon sandbags buffered the base of the lighthouse on the seaside. The beachfront had been renourished several times, and sand fences had been planted to help build up dunes. The most recent effort, I was told, had positioned weighted fronds of artificial seaweed in the ocean to create an offshore sandbar, in hopes of reducing wave erosion.

Efforts to save the Cape Hatteras lighthouse will continue. It has become a symbol of the Outer Banks, of a way of life dependent on the sea. When housing development threatened the surroundings, Cape Hatteras National Seashore was established in 1953; some 75 miles of the Outer Banks became the country's first federally protected shoreline. "For its historic value Cape Hatteras is a national resource that isn't duplicated anywhere else," said Conrad P. Wirth, who served as director of the National Park Service at the time. "Besides its historic value, it's an outstanding piece of shoreline."

North of the national seashore, at Nags Head, a huge pile of sand rises about 135 feet above sea level. Jockey's Ridge is the highest dune on the East Coast. I could easily imagine that I had been transported to the Sahara as I hiked to the top, a forlorn desert rat leaning into the wind and shielding my face as 25-mile-an-hour gusts sent billows of sand swirling around me. Winds constantly sweep the dune, creating a new valley or ridgeline and rearranging hilltops. Vegetation cannot maintain a foothold. Surprisingly, the dune itself remains relatively stable.

"We think this is probably because of the direction of the prevailing winds," said Steve Benton, a geologist with the North Carolina Office of Coastal Management. "From March through August the winds blow southwesterly across the Outer Banks. For the other six months of the year we get northeasterly winds. So the winds are roughly balanced, which may be one reason why Jockey's Ridge is fairly stationary."

It was the steady winds and expansive dunes of the Outer Banks that brought two brothers from Dayton, Ohio, here in 1900 to experiment with flying machines. From the sandy slopes of Kill Devil Hills near the village of Kitty Hawk, Orville and Wilbur Wright made thousands of glider flights to test their theories of aerodynamics. Then on December 17, 1903, Orville revved up the Wright Brothers Flyer, lifted off, and flew 40 yards—man's first successful powered flight in a heavier-than-air machine.

Today man routinely orbits the earth, and from hundreds of miles in space astronauts use the Chesapeake Bay as a visual landmark. The bay is nearly 200 miles long and encompasses

8,000 miles of tidal shoreline. Six major rivers and more than 140 lesser streams feed into the Chesapeake. It is the largest estuary in the United States, a prodigious producer of fish and shellfish. When Capt. John Smith explored the bay in 1608, he recorded an abundance of fish so great that his men "attempted to catch them with a frying pan."

Several colleagues joined me on the Chesapeake one day; we tried our luck not with frying pans but with minnow-baited lines trolled behind a charter boat. Our quarry was striped bass, known locally as rockfish, the most popular commercial and sport fish in the bay—not to be confused with the family of rockfishes on the Pacific coast. For two hours we trolled without a strike. Then the boat passed over a school and within minutes we had seven strikes. By the end of the day we had 24 rockfish, the best haul Capt. Mac McGahey had seen all year.

How did it compare with his best-ever day? "Well, it was years ago, and I usually don't tell people because they don't believe me," Captain Mac replied. "But one day, when we were chumming, we caught 365 rockfish. That was in the morning. In the afternoon we caught 265 more."

It is hard to believe. Rockfish catches in the Chesapeake have declined alarmingly; according to federal researchers, annual harvests dropped from eight million pounds in 1973 to half a million in 1983.

"Rockfish are not reproducing," said L. Eugene Cronin, retired director of the Chesapeake Research Consortium, a coordinating center for studies of the bay. The fish spawn in Chesapeake Bay tributaries, in the upper tidal reaches where the water salinity is low. So conditions in the bay are crucial factors.

"We've dammed many of the tributaries, which means loss of habitat," Cronin asserted. "Also, tremendous amounts of runoff from cities and agricultural lands carry silt, fertilizers, pesticides, and herbicides into the Chesapeake. Factories have dumped toxic chemicals which the bay cannot flush out. And sewage from an increasing population—about 13 million people live in the Chesapeake watershed—puts a burden on the system. The whole load is somehow seriously modifying the environment rockfish re-

quire for spawning. Fishing puts an additional pressure on. Historically, a number of species have been overfished in the bay. Sturgeon was an important staple to the colonies, but sturgeon is virtually gone now. The Chesapeake was once the greatest oystering center in the world, but oyster harvests have also declined. It's very disturbing to see this happen to major fisheries."

Recent studies of spawning streams indicate that acidic water above a certain level kills off the rockfish larvae; but researchers who reported these findings were not certain whether or not acid rain delivered the lethal ingredients.

Before 1976, Chesapeake Bay tributaries spawned 90 percent of the striped bass on the East Coast. Today the proportion is sharply lower. The other major nursery is in the upper reaches of New York's Hudson River. While the northern fishery is holding its own in numbers, there are serious concerns over contamination of the fish by toxic wastes.

In an attempt to increase the population in the Chesapeake, the state of Maryland has issued a ban on the harvesting of rockfish by both commercial and recreational fishermen. Virginia, which has jurisdiction over several major bay tributaries, has reduced its harvest substantially but has not imposed an outright ban. Such steps, said Cronin, constitute "a measure of hope, not of certainty. The bay has received considerable research attention, yet our knowledge is relatively new and still incomplete."

Knowledge. That is the key. The seashore is a mysterious realm, incredibly productive, resilient, yet all too vulnerable. Understanding its vital processes—that is the essence of living with a bay, a beach, or a marsh.

From high above Georgia and South Carolina, an infrared satellite image displays the pattern of a dynamic shorefront. Barrier islands, supporting dune grasses and a coastal forest (the green growth appears red here), absorb the wave action. Behind them simmers the life-giving broth of the wetlands.

FOLLOWING PAGES: *In quiet backwaters flooded twice daily by incoming tides, the salt marsh thrives.*

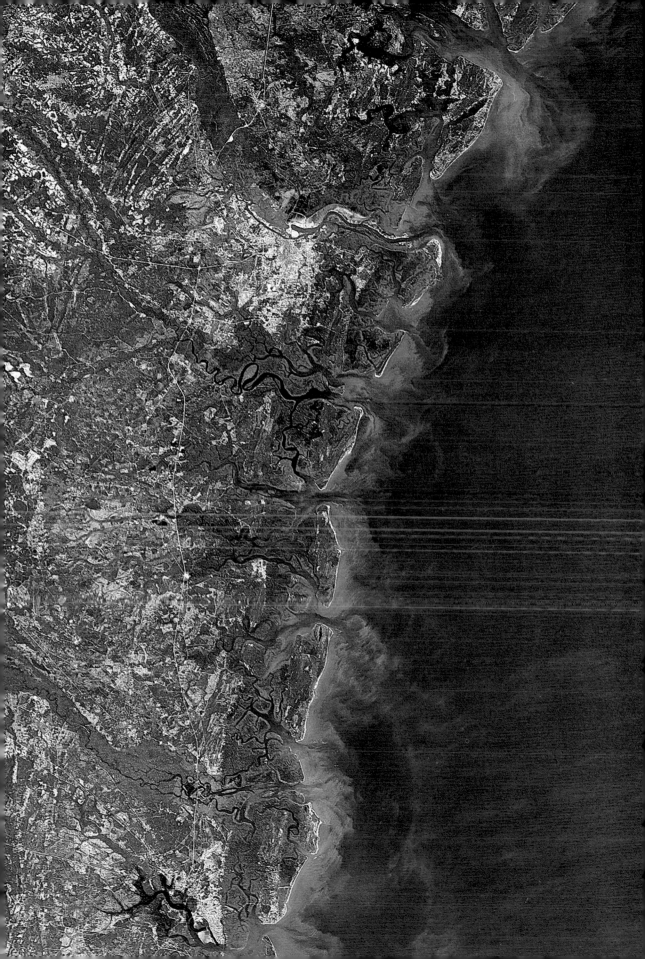

Part land, part sea, the salt marsh encompasses a highly productive ecosystem fueled by decaying plant life. Smooth cordgrass dominates the marsh (opposite); few other plants can survive the daily washing of the tides, the low oxygen level in the soil, and the wide fluctuation in salinity. Low tide brings the tiny fiddler crabs out of their burrows to forage in the mud; at low tide, too, during summer breeding male fiddlers stand outside their burrows and wave a large claw rhythmically to attract females. The courtship ritual resembles the moves of a fiddler briskly sawing on his violin. Soon after mating, the female leaves the burrow and the male resumes his stand, fiddling allegro. The periwinkle snail climbing dead cordgrass (lower right) helps make its own food by shredding the stems. Microorganisms change the shreds into a nutrient-rich detritus for the intricate food web of the marsh. Among the products: algae, food for the periwinkle. At the upland edge, cattails take hold (right); here muskrats find ground cover and, in the cattail roots, nourishment. Long shunned as foul-smelling wastelands, coastal marshes became prime targets for landfill and dredging; nearly half the 11.7 million acres of coastal wetlands in the contiguous 48 states disappeared in the past two centuries. Today coastal management laws seek to preserve the priceless remnants.

FOLLOWING PAGES: Wintering snow geese lift off from a salt marsh at Pea Island National Wildlife Refuge in North Carolina. Wetland habitat accommodates millions of migratory birds along the Atlantic flyway. "Like human travelers," observed Rachel Carson, "birds must have places where they can stop in safety for food and rest." More than 50 national wildlife refuges—including one in Maine that bears Miss Carson's name—preserve such places on the East Coast.

LEFT: JACK DERMID

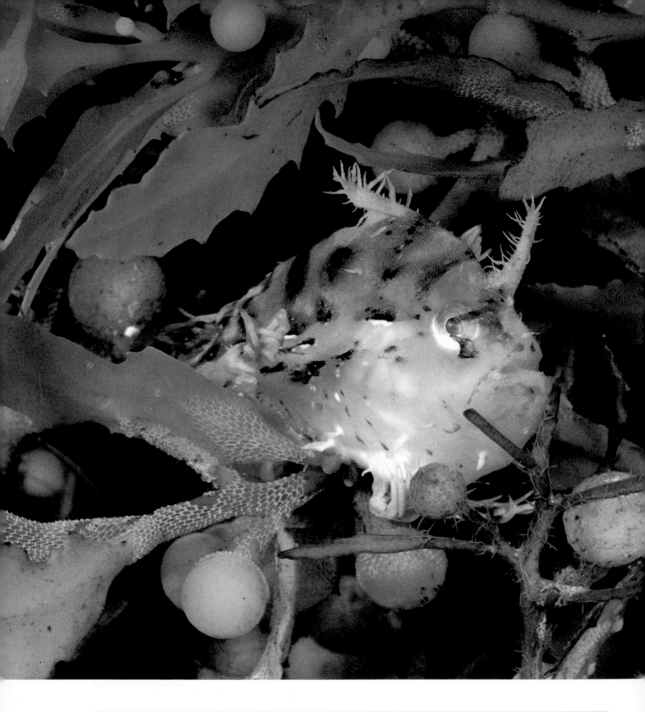

Hidden hunter, a three-inch-long sargassum fish waits for prey to swim by. Leaflike appendages and camouflage colors blend with the weed the fish inhabits. A brown alga, Sargassum—or gulfweed—may, like other seaweeds, attach to rocks along the shore; or it may drift at the ocean's surface, kept afloat by berrylike air bladders. Tiny crabs, shrimp, snails, and the young of many pelagic fishes find food and shelter among the tangle of fronds. Man-made reefs also shelter a huge array of marine life.

A school of tomtates—a species of grunt—nibbles at a barnacled boat (far right), bottomed off the South Carolina coast to improve recreational fishing. Indicating vertical relief on an otherwise flat seafloor, a depth finder (right) pinpoints the artificial reef and its fish for anglers.

FOLLOWING PAGES: Weathering rough surf, fishermen at Cape Hatteras, North Carolina, cast for blues and other fishes migrating close to shore.

ZIG LESZCZYNSKI. BELOW: BOTH BY STEPHEN FRINK

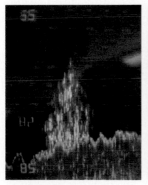

Strollers take the soft, wave-washed side of
a shell-heaped beach near historic Cape Hatteras
Light. Beachcombers seek undamaged shells (far
right) before the waves break them up and grind
them to sand, but the scavenging herring gull (right),
sanitarian of the shore, cares less for the cockleshell
than for the meat inside.

FOLLOWING PAGES: A new day shines on the
Chesapeake; ecologists, watermen, and all who love
seafood dream of a new day for the ailing waters of
the 200-mile-long bay, the nation's largest estuary.

ANIMALS ANIMALS/FRED WHITEHEAD

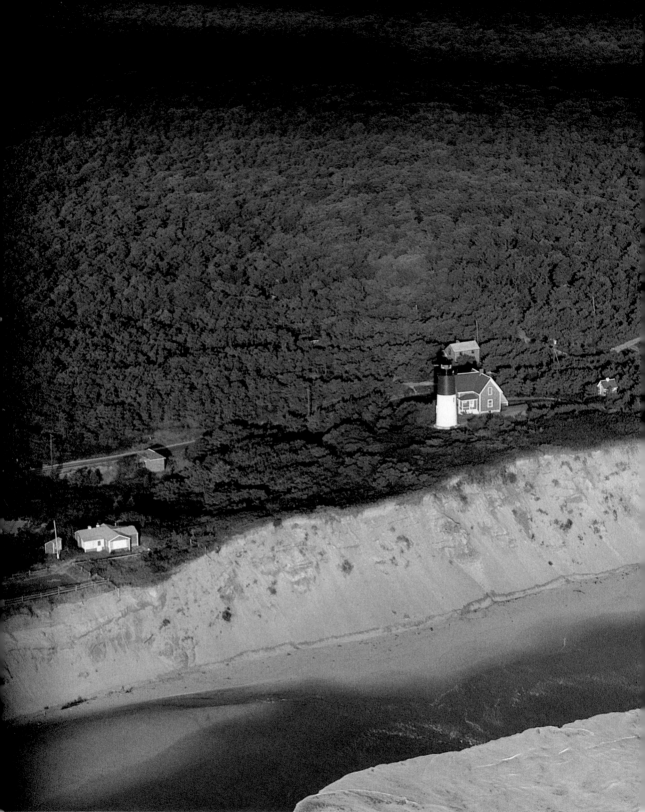

NAUSET LIGHT ATOP THE WAVE-CUT SCARP AT NAUSET BEACH, CAPE COD, MASSACHUSETTS

"On a shore where tidal action is strong . . . one is aware of the ebb and flow of water with a daily, hourly awareness. Each recurrent high tide is a dramatic enactment of the advance of the sea against the continents, pressing up to the very threshold of the land, while the ebbs expose to view a strange and unfamiliar world." RACHEL CARSON

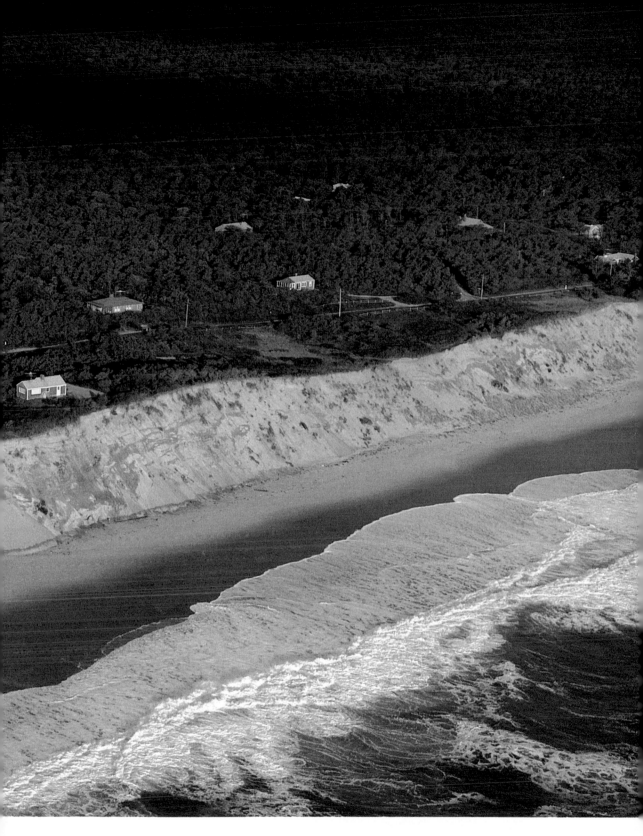

The Northeast

By H. Robert Morrison Photographs by Stephen J. Krasemann

THE HUMPBACK BLEW. A rush of vapor shot skyward and hung in a thin cloud. Then the whale turned and arched its back, a gesture of grace that seemed strange in such an ungainly looking creature. The water swirled and rippled as the curved body, more than 40 feet long, slid downward. The tail, streaming rivulets, broke the surface, then whipped under and disappeared. A circle of roiling sea now marked where the humpback had been.

I looked on from less than a dozen yards away, braced against the rail of a whale-watching boat off Cape Cod. I was in Pilgrim waters, on a pilgrimage along historic shores whose wealth of life had lured European fishing fleets since the 1500s. The northern Atlantic coast was the first to feel the impact and alteration of dense settlement, to receive the outpourings of soaring, populous cities.

And yet the whales are here, so also the landfalls familiar to colonial sailors and even the primeval look of pine forests clinging to granite shores. Precious slivers of unspoiled coast challenge the ingenuity of wilderness guardians, invite scientists to study and comprehend, keep alive the timeless spell that has drawn forth song since the time of Homer.

"Strange!" says Herman Melville in the first pages of *Moby Dick*. "Nothing will content [people] but the extremist limit of the land. . . . They must get just as nigh the water as they possibly can without falling in."

A headspring of Walt Whitman's inspiration was Paumanok, the name he used for Long Island: "Starting from fish-shape Paumanok where I was born. . . ." In 1849 Henry David Thoreau reached the Atlantic side of Cape Cod on foot. An inlander, he stood astounded at the elemental "force of the ocean stream. . . . the breakers looked like droves of a thousand wild horses of Neptune, rushing to the shore, with their white manes streaming far behind."

I too, trod the sands of Paumanok, saw the white-maned horses of Cape Cod, and continued north until I watched earth's most awesome tides fill Canada's Bay of Fundy.

My journey began one early October day on the crest of a sand dune near the southern tip of New Jersey. Just a bit north the historic resort of Cape May proudly flaunts its Victoriana, gingerbread streetscapes that look as if they had been inspired by *New Yorker* covers. A mile to the south, where New Jersey ends, migrating birds in the fall must brave 14 miles of open water at the mouth of Delaware Bay. Not surprisingly, birds tend to tarry here. So do people, to see the songbirds passing through, but especially to see the spectacular passage of hawks that hunt the small birds and rodents and insects before moving on. In autumn the cape is hawk-watchers' heaven.

Years ago the hawks attracted hunters. Ornithologist Witmer Stone described the autumnal slaughter in his *Bird Studies at Old Cape May*: "The bombardment begins as soon as it is light enough to see. . . . so frequent are the discharges that it actually sounds as if some sort of engagement or mock battle were in progress."

The hawking guns have been stilled. I watched the sun come up and heard only the whispering of birders, bird calls, and the fluttering of warblers, sparrows, and flickers in the cedar and scrubby wax myrtle. Suddenly a winged hunter swooped in low. I caught it in the glasses: a sharp-shinned hawk. Another sharpie, borne on an updraft, popped over a bush a few yards away. The close encounter startled us both.

I moved on to nearby Cape May Point State Park and joined members of the New Jersey Audubon Society for their annual autumn weekend at the cape. They were an interesting mix: affluent old-timers garbed in explorer chic; young parents backpacking toddlers; earnest novices fidgeting with brand-new binoculars. The birds were the stars of this drama, but as wave after wave flew past or circled overhead, even the most dedicated birder couldn't maintain the first flush of enthusiasm. "What's that?" "Peregrine." "Oh. Just another peregrine."

Since 1976 the society's Cape May Bird Observatory has kept a daily tally of the fall hawk migration—or at least as much of it as a single observer can spot on a long watch that begins at dawn. Though the count has never broken a hundred thousand, observatory director Peter Dunne estimates the seasonal total at more than twice that number. Sharpshins outnumber all other species by far. A cold front, accompanied by northwest winds that push the migrants out to sea, makes a Delaware Bay crossing especially risky. Under such conditions the birds gather at the cape in incredible numbers, producing delightful "days of madness" for birders. On October 4, 1977, after five days of no-go weather, the count soared to 21,800, including 11,000 sharpshins and 9,400 broad-winged hawks. That one-day record has not been topped.

A short stroll from the hawk-watch platform at the state park takes visitors to a pleasant viewpoint atop the weathered concrete hulk known as the bunker. A World War II coastal defense battery, weighing thousands of tons with walls six feet thick, the bunker was built to last. But it won't. Once it stood 900 feet from the shore, its pilings and roof mounded with earth. Today it stands in the surf, its slender pilings exposed. A park sign asks: How long can the pilings support the bunker? Visitors are left to wonder.

The story begins in 1911, when the Army Engineers built thousand-foot-long jetties to keep Cold Spring Inlet from sanding up. Soon the beaches just to the south—the beaches of Cape May City and South Cape May—began to starve. Storm and erosion took their sand; the jetties blocked replenishing drift. In time Cape May City built a series of groins and took other steps to preserve the precious strand. From the bunker you can see the handsome resort, with its beach and its jetties. But what of South Cape May, less than a mile away? The town lacked the wherewithal, financial and political, says a local planner, to protect its shorefront. The houses are gone. The townsite is underwater—"the little town that was."

Accessible to more millions of people than any other segment of the continental shore, the megalopolis coast yet retains landforms and life forms of its primal past. Whales haunt its coves, birds use it as a migration road map—and rest stop and seasonal resort as well. Though many a marsh lies buried under concrete, the tides still wash wild headlands and untrammeled sands, and in Canada's Bay of Fundy rise higher than anywhere else in the world.

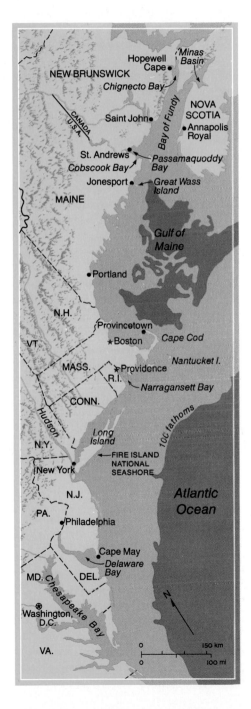

Beyond the northern edge of New Jersey we begin to see the handiwork of the Ice Age glaciers: Long Island, Cape Cod, Martha's Vineyard, Nantucket—ridges of mixed sand and rock scraped from the continent like the curl a toy bulldozer pushes along a sandbox. The array of life changes as the warm ocean river of the Gulf Stream angles eastward into the Atlantic. Cape Cod, at the northern edge of the current, becomes a kind of thermal fence, dividing warm-water species from cold. But as northern waters have felt the warming trend of recent times, southern species have passed through the fence. Since the beginning of this century, for example, the green crab has extended its range from the cape to Passamaquoddy Bay and Nova Scotia.

The glacier-scoured northern shores are rockier, and support a richer growth of seaweeds and intertidal life than does the soft unglaciated shorefront. North of Cape Cod the deepfreeze of winter grips the salt marshes; the ice scouring of spring breakup can devastate a marsh for years.

In earlier days rural folk prized the marsh grasses—the cordgrass, *Spartina alterniflora*, for thatch, and the shorter salt hay, *Spartina patens*, for fodder. Marsh Day in September marked the harvest time, the horses fitted with wooden shoes to keep them from sinking in the spongy ground. In the 17th century, New Hampshire-men railed against the cropping of their salt hay by armed invaders from Massachusetts. In Boston the Back Bay wetlands of the Charles River were scorned as a "stinking eyesore"; drained and filled, they became the foundation for a "new heart of the city" with museums, concert halls, libraries. Scarcely a trace of the wetlands survives, though a hint of the old marshes, or fens, lives on along the Back Bay Fens and in the name of the Red Sox stadium, Fenway Park.

So went our expanding cities and suburbs, heedless, in the main, of the cost to the natural community. Times change. Westway, a multi-billion-dollar project in New York City, was stymied for years—by young striped bass. Born in the upper reaches of the Hudson River, the stripers spend their first winter around lower Manhattan, exactly where Westway planners wanted a landfill for a stretch of superhighway, centerpiece of the development. The new skyline remained a vision as environmentalists—some admitting they hated Westway more than they loved the fish—pleaded the cause of the striper through the bureaucracy and the courts. In 1985 a deadline for funding passed, and Westway died.

No wildlife is too small to escape the attention of preservationists and nature students, even mosquitoes. Out on Fire Island National Seashore—off the south shore of Long Island, at about the belly of Walt Whitman's fish shape—I found the beaches teeming with vacationers and, yes, mosquitoes.

There exists no more passionate enmity than that between man and mosquito. Yet Jack Hauptmann, superintendent of the national seashore, looks out for the interests of both. The traditional weaponry—spraying and other control measures—is deployed through Fire Island's 17 communities, totaling some 4,000 houses. But the 32-mile-long barrier island also includes the gnarled, 300-year-old holly trees of the Sunken Forest, along with shadblow and tupelo and sassafras, catbrier, wild grape, and masses of poison ivy. "Those hollies are our redwoods," notes Hauptmann. There are also the marshes, with their cordgrass and salt hay, and the tree swallows swooping to and fro over the fecund mosquito nurseries, dining on the wing.

An eight-mile strip of the seashore is a designated wilderness area. There, says Hauptmann, "we don't spray—and we don't want to." But what if mosquitoes from the wilderness breeding sites are migrating to Long Island and feeding on suburbanites?

Entomologist Howard Ginsberg was trying to gauge the size of the problem, and I joined him one day in a four-wheel-drive vehicle, growling slowly eastward toward the marsh. Only National Park Service and workers' vehicles are allowed on the seashore in summer; the few visiting motorists able to get permits even to drive to the island must park outside the preserve and walk in.

"We are mainly concerned with one species, *Aedes sollicitans,* the striped salt marsh mosquito," said Howard as we approached the study site. "It's by far the most numerous mosquito, and it breeds in the salt marshes of Fire Island. Also, we're mainly concerned with the females, because they're the ones that bite people. The males eat plant juices, and so do the females. But in order to lay eggs, the females need proteins from the blood of warm-blooded animals."

Like us. They began attacking at the edge of the marsh. We used no repellent—it might contaminate the mosquito traps. Our only defense was the brush-off. An ingenious rig is used to catch the insects. A battery-powered light attracts mosquitoes to the mouth of the trap, and a fan sucks them in. Dry ice hangs nearby; as it evaporates it releases carbon dioxide, mimicking the breath of animals—a special bait for the females.

A fluorescent powder—a different color for each site—marks the trapped insects. Then they're released. Those that are caught again provide some idea of where the island's mosquitoes go. "We've caught very few Fire Island insects on Long Island proper," said Howard. "So far, it looks like only a small percentage from the wilderness is migrating inland, which should be welcome news to Long Islanders." Welcome news, also, for those who like the idea of a truce between man and the mosquito.

The wilderness preserves a bit of Fire Island as it must have appeared to the first Europeans to visit here four centuries ago. For many an immigrant dreaming of a new life, the first glimpse of the New World was of the Fire Island Light at Great South Bay. Whale oil, lard oil, kerosene, oil vapor, and electricity lit lighthouse beacons here until a decade ago. But a volunteer group sparked a drive to relight the darkened tower. It is scheduled to shine forth again in 1986, when the restored Statue of Liberty rekindles her torch of welcome in New York harbor, just to the west.

Later, the heat and insects of Fire Island seemed far away on a September afternoon in Rhode Island's Narragansett Bay. Covering 174 square miles from Providence at its head to Aquidneck Island at its mouth, the bay has been the subject of estuarine research for generations. Much of that research has centered on pollution.

Providence was prominent in the Industrial Revolution that swept New England in the 19th century. A report to Rhode Island's General Assembly in 1895 estimated that Providence industries improvidently dumped six million gallons of factory wastes and 25 tons of grease into tributaries of the bay daily. But the city also led the nation in sewage treatment. Its Fields Point plant, designed in 1897, was a model for the time.

However, that original plant is still in operation, along with other overtaxed facilities that periodically discharge raw sewage into Narragansett Bay. The Providence sewer system channels rainwater through the treatment plants, creating an influx greater than they can handle.

At the University of Rhode Island's Graduate School of Oceanography, researcher Barbara Nowicki brought me up to date. "It's a very complex system," she said. "Besides the inflow from overwhelmed sewage plants, there's runoff from farming activities and bayside construction. Water enters the bay both from rivers and from the ocean. This complicates tracing the flow of pollutants. And many factors, such as sunlight and temperature, vary with the seasons. And we don't know how long pollutants remain harmful in the bottom sediments. If we eliminated all pollutants flowing into the bay tomorrow, would the water quality improve, or would the effects of past dumping keep the bay polluted?"

When I visited the bay, Barbara's research was focused on the production and consumption of oxygen, an important agent in photosynthesis and the food chain. In summer, oxygen levels drop sharply in the upper bay and the estuary of the Providence River, with a resulting die-off of fish, shellfish, and crustaceans. Barbara was trying to determine just where the oxygen deficit was occurring.

I explored one aspect of her research the following day, when technicians Jenny Martin and Jim McKenna took me for a spin over the choppy waters. At several stations in the upper bay and the mouths of rivers we filled clear flasks and dark flasks and hung them from floats at set depths. Sunlight would enter the clear flasks, allowing phytoplankton to produce oxygen, while other organisms consumed it. In the dark flasks oxygen would be consumed *(Continued on page 157)*

Watching or watched, the autumn Capers are all eyes. Demonstrating its keen outlook—a family trait in a tribe of aerial hunters—a peregrine falcon halts briefly at Cape May, New Jersey, before resuming its southward peregrination. The Cape gives pause to the migrants, many of them inexperienced young songbirds and hawks on their first long-range flight, for here they must cross the gaping mouth of Delaware Bay. Birders also gather here, especially on October weekends, packing the historic resort nearby and enjoying the vantage of the counting site at Cape May Point (below). Compiling data for conservation programs, a counter mans the platform from August to December. Some migrants, like the falcon at right, are netted for banding. Sharpshin numbers invariably lead the list. Kestrels, merlins, harriers, ospreys, and Cooper's and red-tailed hawks make a good showing. Arctic peregrines number in the hundreds—a normal population, doubled in size since DDT was banned in 1972.

Creatures of the deep, finback and humpback summer in nearshore waters of New England and Canada, where researchers study and whale-watchers enjoy their antics. Head down, telltale dorsal fin sticking up, a finback (above) begins a dive in Passamaquoddy Bay. Reaching as much as 70 feet in length, second only to the blue whales in size, the finbacks show themselves often.

But the more gregarious and acrobatic humpbacks put on a better show. Off Cape Cod one bolts up, to the delight of nearby observers. Winglike flippers gave the humpback its scientific name: Megaptera novaeangliae, big-winged New Englander.

but not produced. By comparing the two it would be possible to measure oxygen productivity at each site under given light conditions.

We finished the rounds only in time to spin around and collect the flasks. When I remarked on the drudgery, Jenny laughed. "If you think this is tedious," she said, "you ought to see us in the lab. It will take a couple of days to process the 80 bottles we're bringing back today. Imagine running the same chemical test 80 times." What makes it worthwhile, she continued, is that her work adds to the growing body of knowledge about estuaries—how they can be used for man's needs and still remain viable ecosystems.

Cape Cod juts into the sea from southeastern Massachusetts like an arm bent at the elbow, with the fist curled, making a muscle. At the fingertips lies Provincetown, home of the Center for Coastal Studies.

"Provincetown's an extraordinarily good spot for whale-watching," said Charles A. Mayo, director of the center. "In summer you can see whales from the beach here three days out of four. Moreover, a group of humpback whales has an intense affinity for this area. We've documented the fact that more than 90 percent of the group returns here year after year. That means we have a stable population of about 190 animals. We give each animal a name, usually based on some distinctive marking, to help us remember individuals. On sighting a whale, we can almost always identify it from memory.

"We've been able to cooperate with the commercial whale-watching boats in Province-town. Our observers serve as guides on the boats. That lets us get out four times a day, weather per-

mitting, without the expense of running our own boat. That's really important." As part of the research team, observer-guides are able to collect valuable data while they are out with visitors.

In recent years, as the campaign against the commercial killing of whales intensified, whale-watching emerged as a symbol of environmental concern, of support for the beleaguered sea mammals. Hundreds of thousands board whale-watching boats from New England to Hawaii. Now the fear grows that heavy boat traffic disturbs whales by disrupting feeding or mating.

Mayo regards the issue as a serious one. These are endangered animals, and every precaution must be taken to shield them. "Except for the gray whales of Baja California," he points out, "our whales are the most whale-watched whales in the world." The animals are surely aware of the boats, Mayo adds, but so far there's no sign—to human observers, at any rate—of any serious disruption in the life of the whales.

Aboard the *Dolphin IV* researcher Carole Carlson picked up a microphone and pointed out a female and her calf to the whale-watchers. "This is Columbia," Carole said. "We first photographed her in 1980, and she's returned every year since then. Oftentimes she's been spotted with Orion, a male. This year, though, is the first time we've seen her with a calf. We haven't named the calf yet." I was amazed that we could approach within 50 yards of these wild creatures. Columbia and her calf didn't swim away and didn't seem at all alarmed.

I was hoping to see the whale named Navaho. I had "adopted" it through the Whale Adoption Project, which helps raise funds for the center. For a modest donation I had received a photograph of Navaho (marked below its dorsal fin vaguely like the pattern of an Indian rug, hence the name). A certificate proclaimed me an Official Protector of Navaho. I had become concerned when a newsletter mentioned that my adoptee hadn't been seen in 1983.

"Navaho appears to be a loner," Carole told me. "We don't see it nearly as often as we do most of these whales. In fact, we don't know yet whether Navaho is male or female. But this year it was sighted swimming with one of our whales off Puerto Rico."

Another spring, another spawning melee of horseshoe crabs on a New Jersey shore. During the mating ritual, each female deposits and buries thousands of eggs; then males and females return to sea. Weeks later, a new generation breaks out of the sands and heads for the water, as the species extends a saga of survival that began some 360 million years ago. On Delaware Bay beaches, horseshoe crab eggs exposed by the surf provide sustenance for a giant staging area of northbound shorebirds.

Although I didn't see "my" whale, I was glad to know that Navaho was still alive. And I did come away with one imperishable memory, when—no more than ten yards from the boat— a mighty spout shot up and a majestic humpback sounded, leaving only a circular "tailprint" of roiling water.

For more than a decade the center has studied the group of humpbacks, adding some 20,000 photographs each year, recording the lineages of new calves and gathering knowledge of feeding and social behavior. The humpbacks arrive in spring, stay for about eight months, and head south in November or December. Food is probably the primary lure that brings them back to these waters year after year; a staple of their diet is the sand lance, the eel-like fish that can burrow into sand and mud to ride out low tide or avoid predators. Mayo suspects there may also be some social imperative that draws the humpbacks back to familiar summer haunts: "They know this habitat like we know our backyards."

Just before they depart, he continues, the humpbacks begin to sing. The melodies are identical to the haunting songs of the humpbacks recorded in southern waters where they mate.

Ongoing efforts to save the world's whales contrast sharply with the callous extermination of the great auk in the 19th century. This large, flightless seabird was once fairly common in Cape Cod waters and along the coast in both directions, being reported in ship's logs as far back as Jacques Cartier in 1534.

For men with clubs or oars the great auk was easy prey, and European mariners quickly exploited this rich source of provision. Sailors took dories and filled them with dead birds. In 1622 it seemed evident to Sir Richard Whitbourne that "God made the innocency of so poor a creature to become an admirable instrument for the sustenation of man." The slaughter continued generation after generation. The last great auk on Cape Cod was killed sometime in the 1830s; shortly thereafter the species was extinct.

North of the cape, along the "stern and rock-bound coast" of poetry, spreads a profusion of islands, hardy outcroppings isolated from the mainland when melting ice raised the level of the sea. On a sunny September day I visited one of

them to explore a unique coastal environment.

The Nature Conservancy owns about half of Great Wass Island, off Jonesport, Maine, and manages its 1,500 acres as a preserve to protect a number of plant communities rare in Maine. I set off with Charles Richards, retired professor of botany at the University of Maine, as my guide. Along the trail bushy sheep laurel grew thick under red and black spruces and balsam firs. A few barely ripened mountain cranberries begged us to taste them. A leaf plucked from a shrub and crumpled in my companion's hand wafted the fragrance of sweet gale in my direction.

The trail climbed to a stand of jack pines, one of the largest stands of the species in Maine. The trees were stunted and twisted, like bonsais, their exposed roots grasping at granite boulders and ledges. "This soil is only a couple of inches thick in most places," Richards explained. "Few other trees can grow here, so the jack pines have little competition.

"Jack pines usually need fire to regenerate. Their cones stay closed until they're heated, when they open and release seeds. But these are different, evidently, because you can see young jack pine seedlings throughout this stand— though it hasn't burned for at least 70 years."

Farther along, we stood near the edge of a level, open expanse of about five acres, with only a scrubby jack pine struggling here and there.

"This is a plateau bog," the professor said. "It's different from most bogs, which are formed by vegetation gradually filling ponds until the open water disappears. This bog formed over a base of mud. It was wet enough to grow sphagnum moss, which partially decayed into peat. These plants are growing on a layer of peat several feet thick."

Since peat is poor in nutrients, he went on, most of the bog plants are ombrotrophic; that means they get needed nutrients not from ground water, as most plants do, but from rain and airborne particles. I would have guessed that vegetation growing under such adverse conditions would be sparse. But when we walked onto the bog, the resilient peat springing with each footstep, tiny plants covered every inch. Richards bent down and pointed out several: "Here's a small bog cranberry—only about half the size of the common bog cranberry. That's bog golden-rod, again a miniature. Here's a black crowberry; it's common in the Arctic, but rare this far south. This one is baked apple berry—a member of the rose family whose single yellow berry really does taste like a baked apple."

Leapfrogging along the coast, I landed next at Lubec, a Maine border town where the New England Aquarium conducts a study of the right whale—the most endangered whale species in the world. Its name was also a death warrant, because whalers centuries ago learned that it was the "right" whale to kill. Right whales often swam near the shore, and could be hunted in small land-based boats. At sea they were easily approached and were relatively slow swimmers. They floated when killed. A single large animal might yield 150 barrels of oil and half a ton of valuable whalebone.

By the mid-1700s too few right whales were left to sustain the North Atlantic fishery, and whalers turned to more distant seas. By the 1930s so few right whales remained that whaling nations gave them worldwide protection.

Aboard the research vessel *Nereid*, I asked Scott Kraus how the right whale study in the lower Bay of Fundy originated. "It started sort of by accident," he recalled. "In 1980 we were here doing experiments to determine the best way to survey harbor porpoises—by land, air, water. An oil company had proposed a big refinery at East-port just across the mouth of Cobscook Bay. However, their environmental impact statement said nothing much about marine mammals. So the National Marine Fisheries Service contract-ed with the New England Aquarium to survey the summer population of marine mammals in the lower Bay of Fundy.

"We found a lot, including minke and pilot whales and endangered species—humpbacks and finbacks. But our biggest discovery was con-sistent numbers of right whales. That summer we identified through photographs 26 individual right whales. At the time, it was estimated that only about 100 of the animals remained in the North Atlantic. Here we had found what we thought then was a quarter of the population! And among them were four cow-calf pairs—all the recruitment to the population that anyone knew about."

Scott paused to point out a V-shaped twin spout—the telltale sign of the right whale. "Strange," he continued, "we still don't know, after half a century of total worldwide protection, whether or not the numbers of this most threat-ened whale are increasing or decreasing. Until this spring we didn't even know where the fe-males went to bear their young. Then we discov-ered 15 right whales, including four cow-calf pairs, during aerial surveys along the coasts of Georgia and Florida last February. But that ac-counts for only a few; where do the rest go?"

Although scientists also do not understand fully what makes the Bay of Fundy attractive to right whales, they point out that the bay provides a bounty of tiny organisms for the whales to eat.

"How productive is the Bay of Fundy?" Da-vid Scarratt, then acting director of the Fisheries and Marine Service Biological Station at St. An-drews, New Brunswick, repeated my question. "We harvest 50,000 tons of sardine-size herring each year. Compare that with the annual catch of 120,000 tons of fish of all species taken from the much larger fishing grounds of Georges Bank. There's good scalloping, clamming, and lobstering here, too. We've got deep, deep up-wellings in the bay that bring nutrients to the surface. It's a very dynamic system."

The Bay of Fundy's dynamic that perennial-ly captures the world's attention is its tides. In Minas Basin, the eastern arm at the head of the bay, the difference between high tide and low tide sometimes exceeds 52 feet. When I asked Scarratt why the bay has such great tides, he in-vited me to a lecture he was giving to students visiting St. Andrews on a field trip.

He began by explaining how the changing positions of sun and moon produce the highest and lowest tides each month—the spring and neap tides. "You might visualize the tides as a pair of large waves," he added, "one on each side of the globe and circling the earth about every

12½ hours. The water itself doesn't move much, just the energy of the wave.

"There are two main reasons why the tides here are so high, and both of them relate to the size and shape of the bay. The simpler reason is that the bay gets progressively shallower and narrower. A given amount of water will create greater differences in a shallower basin, and indeed the greatest tides are found at the head of the bay. To understand the other, more complex reason, you have to understand the principle of resonance. An example will show what I mean.

"Think of pushing someone in a swing. If your pushes are timed to match the swing, tiny pushes can add up to make the swing go higher and higher. What you're doing is matching the resonance of the swing's arc. Something similar happens in the Bay of Fundy.

"In any basin, the time it takes a wave to move from end to end and back again is the natural period of the basin. Fundy and the Gulf of Maine together have a period of 12 hours and 45 minutes—very close to the tidal period of 12 hours, 25 minutes. So, like rhythmically pushing a swing, the ocean tides arrive at intervals that reinforce the gulf and bay tidal rhythm, thus increasing the tidal amplitude."

Scarratt also discussed the use of the tides to generate electricity—a subject of special interest here. Even while I visited, North America's first tidal generating plant was nearing completion at Annapolis Royal, Nova Scotia. "Compared with the alternatives—burning coal or oil or using nuclear energy," Scarratt said, "tidal power sounds like an attractive means to generate electricity. But it is more complicated than it seems."

Tidal power projects include dams. "By damming off parts of the bay," said Scarratt, "you decrease its natural period. That would make it even closer to the period of the ocean tides, increasing tidal amplitude throughout the Gulf of Maine and the Bay of Fundy. As scientists we don't know fully the effects this might cause, so we must be very careful."

Other scientists studying the problem with computer models have estimated that tidal power dams under construction would cause high tides along the coast of Maine to be six inches higher and low tides six inches lower. Such a change, predicts one researcher, would cause the loss of more than 4,000 acres of coastal property.

The significance of predictions like these is much in dispute; and there is also concern for the ecological integrity of the great bay. New studies, spurred by the power proposals, revealed an abundance of life far beyond expectations in the turbulent, muddy upper bay. Each summer, for example, some 14 million shad migrate through there. And the algae covering the mud flats feed enormous quantities of an amphipod known as mud shrimp, a food source for millions of migratory shorebirds. Would development of hydroelectricity affect such populations? Clearly, as Dave Scarratt suggested, tidal power in the Bay of Fundy is a complex issue.

One of the best places to see the power of these tides is Hopewell Cape on Chignecto Bay, Fundy's western arm. Here ice, rain, streams, and 45-foot tides have cut strange formations in soft sandstone filled with pebbles and boulders. The tide was falling as I climbed down from the cliff top and tramped along the wet sand. Towering four stories above me, the mushroom shapes of the weathered rock made me feel like a pixie wandering a springtime wood. I walked through a natural archway and pulled back some sea wrack to search for tiny whelks. In a dank cave I ran my hand over the rough wall.

Watching the tide retreat, I realized my brief encounter with "the extremist limit of the land" was ending. I remembered the tiny mosquitoes and the fierce birds of prey, 40-foot whales and barnacles smaller than my fingertips, estuaries burdened with the wastes of cities and a breeze-swept, pristine beach. Incredible contrasts. Wondrous shores.

Not a ripple disturbs the reflection of a lesser yellowlegs in Cape Cod's Wellfleet Bay Sanctuary. This shorebird usually avoids outer shores, probing for crustaceans on mud flats; its larger relative, the greater yellowlegs, chases fish in marsh pools. In the days before protection, when gunners stalked the marshes spring and fall, the yellowlegs earned the nickname "telltale," for they were quick to sound the alarm to their neighbors in the wetlands.

Cape Cod, once forested, started giving up its trees for fuel and housing when the Pilgrims landed. As land was denuded, formerly stable dunes began moving. Fences slow the sands (left); planted beach grass (above) holds them. Pines planted 75 years ago to protect Provincetown now lie engulfed (below).

In the interest of conservation Cape Cod National Seashore banned visitor nudity, fearing that gawkers would trample the dunes.

PRECEDING PAGES· At the fist of Cape Cod, wave-borne and windblown sands shape the Province Lands.

Reversing falls of Cobscook Bay: Incoming tides rush over a rocky ledge toward land, while the ebbs spill seaward. Cobscook lies in Maine on the southwestern edge of Canada's Bay of Fundy, a sleeve-shaped, 170-mile-long indentation that engenders earth's most extreme tidal variations— the highest tides could flood a five-story building.

In Minas Basin, on the Nova Scotia side, low tide grounds a boat and empties the cove at Parrsboro.

FOLLOWING PAGES: Low water bares the Hopewell Rocks in New Brunswick, where sandstone 330 million years old slowly yields to the artistry of Fundy tides and weathering.

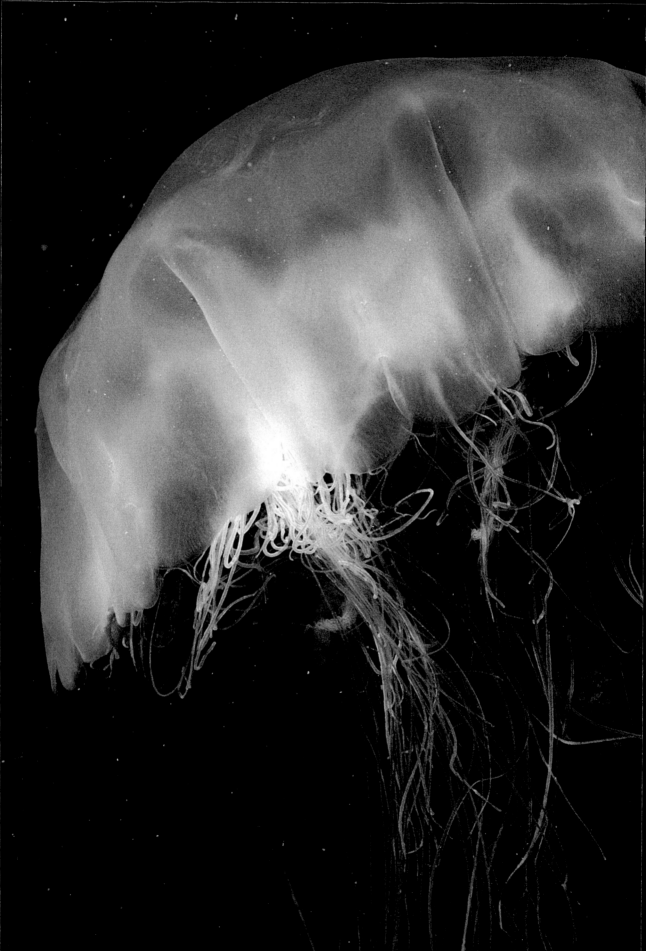

Largest of all jellyfish, the lion's mane (left) may grow a bell three feet in diameter in the Gulf of Maine. But rare arctic giants may measure eight feet across, the tentacles stretching 200 feet. Predator of the intertidal, the smooth sun star (below) dines on small starfish and sea cucumbers. "Collapsing forest" of knotted rockweed—an alga—lies draped on the rocks of Cobscook Bay at low tide (right); air bladders float it upright in high water.

FOLLOWING PAGES: Tentacles of a scarlet sea cucumber comb intertidal waters, bringing plankton and detritus to the mouth of the tubular body.

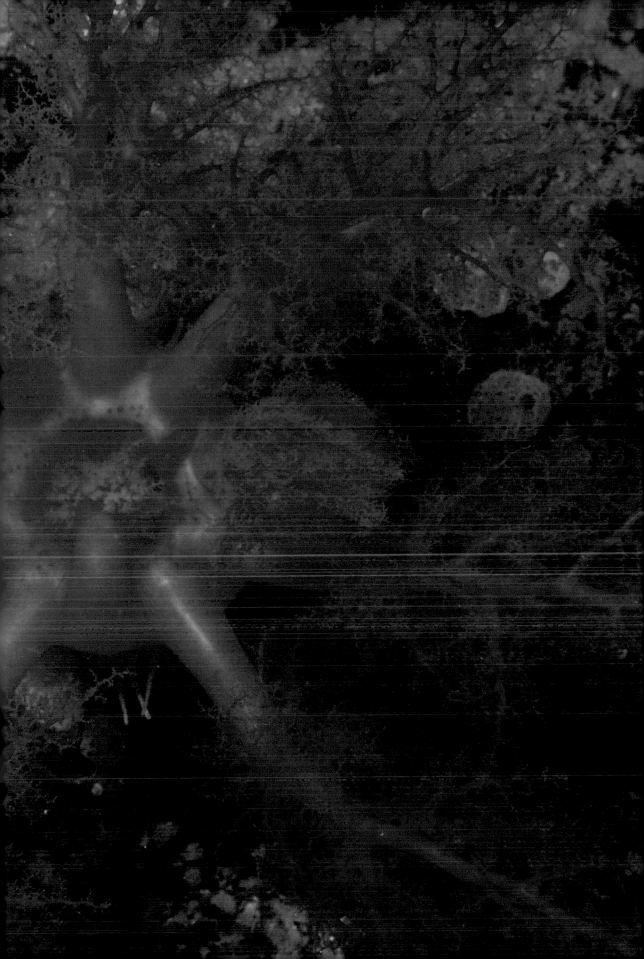

Fog softens Maine's "stern and rock-bound coast." Before radar, the dark hues of this granite cliff oriented Jonesport boatmen groping through the soup for home. "We'd be makin'—as we say it here—each point very slowly, soundin' all the way," says Capt. Barna Norton. "Dark granite here meant we were east of Jonesport; pink'd be to the west." Formed when warm moist air moves offshore, fog sets foghorns wailing, helps cool the coast, shades aquatic life exposed at low tide, and makes the woodlands at the edge more fire resistant than inland forests. At times heavy seas send waves crashing against the cliffs, the salt spray dousing trees within range. Bois Bubert Island (below) reveals another facet of the sea's power. Here storm waves heaped up stones to build a natural seawall and cobble beach, turning a cove into a pond, where black ducks breed and bald eagles hunt.

FOLLOWING PAGES: Wintry West Quoddy Head marks Maine's farthest east; its lighthouse, stripped of paint for a cleaning, has since received a new coat of its familiar barber pole striping. East Quoddy Head lies farther east—but on Canada's Campobello Island in the distance.

The Virgin Islands

TINY EMERALDS in a crystal sea, the U.S. Virgin Islands add a special luster to the seashores of America. Glittering in transparent waters, the islands of St. Thomas, St. John, and St. Croix conjure travel-poster visions of powdery sands under a lush canopy of green. Such beaches abound in the Virgin Islands, thanks to a delicately balanced set of conditions.

Vital to the islands' sandy shores are the coral reefs that thrive in startling variety in the warm, clear, sunlit waters of the Caribbean rim. These formations are continuously broken up by wave action and converted into sand by browsing sea creatures such as the parrotfish. Waves and currents sweep the sediments to the nearby shores, constantly replenishing the sand carried off by wind or backwash.

Two basic types of reef formations are found in the islands. Fringing reefs grow near the shoreline, while patch reefs grow in deeper water amid the sea grasses and algae that flourish on the sandy seafloor.

Not only does the fringing coral supply sand to island beaches, but it also helps protect coastal areas from erosion by blunting the force of waves. Even during hurricanes, fringing reefs greatly reduce damage to the inner shore.

Fantasy shapes of elkhorn coral, top, brain coral, middle, and lettuce coral, lower, brighten the waters off St. Croix. Home to abundant sea life, such reefs shield the shores of the Virgin Islands.

FOLLOWING PAGES: Snorkelers explore lava-bordered Turtle Bay in the national park on St. John, vacation mecca for thousands.

PAGES 182-83: Young mangroves venture into the shallows of Leinster Bay on St. John. Usually mangroves help expand a swampland, but storm surf here will uproot the pioneers.

The reefs include such common hard corals as the wildly branching elkhorn and staghorn, as well as star, pillar, brain, lettuce, and fire corals. Here, too, are the soft corals, or gorgonians: the sea whips, sea plumes, and sea fans that undulate gracefully in the currents.

Differing methods of growth produce the variations in shape among the coral colonies. In some species, individual coral polyps multiply by dividing; in others, new polyps branch off old ones. Even within a single species, colonies vary in appearance in response to environmental conditions: Strong currents tend to produce more massive formations than do quieter waters.

The reefs are home to an amazing array of life. Brightly colored fish hover near these underwater hotels. Sponges, anemones, feather duster worms, cowries, sea urchins, shrimp, and lobsters are also guests.

Moray eels lurk in their nooks. Nurse sharks cruise lethargically, while schooling fish dash here and there in a sort of synchronized frenzy. Rare sea turtles —the hawksbill, leatherback, and green sea turtle—also inhabit the reefs, feeding on grasses growing nearby.

Not all island shores are edged with sand. Off steeper areas, corals grow in deeper water and waves pound the shore with greater force. Here the beach may be covered with smooth stones and chunks of coral. Below windward headlands, where heavy seas are common, large, jagged boulders form a jumbled shoreline.

Volcanic in origin, the Virgin Islands still bear signs of their birth. At Nanny Point, on the east shore of St. John, the sea buffets volcanic rock formed a hundred million years ago. On the north coast, small beaches are covered by dark-blue cobbles, weathered volcanic fragments.

Some 7,000 acres of St. John—two-thirds of its land—and 5,600 acres of its surrounding waters have been set aside as Virgin Islands National Park. Within the sanctuary lie some of the loveliest beaches in the world.

Hawaii

BLUE WATER ROILS to a white frenzy as waves break in a curl of surf off Hawaii's Black Sand Beach. Their energy spent, the waves fan out across the glistening shore, ending in lacy scallops of foam. To those who stroll here, these ebony sands offer more than striking beauty; their color speaks of the volcanic legacy of the islands.

For eons, lava has periodically poured into the sea on this southeastern shore of the Big Island. Chilled by the water, the lava shatters. At once waves attack the fragments, eventually grating them into fine-textured sand.

Other Big Island beaches tell equally colorful tales. Near Hawaii's southern tip, the mineral olivine tints sands a distinctive green; powdery sands of shell and coral produce shimmering white beaches on the western Kona coast.

The Big Island's 313-mile shoreline presents still greater contrasts. Sands give way to lava palisades, craggy shoulders thrusting into the restive sea. Lofty ridges, kept lush by moisture in the trade winds from the northeast, shield stream-cut valleys of incredible beauty.

Youngest isle in the 1,500-mile Hawaiian chain, the Big Island is still growing. Eruptions of Kilauea Volcano continue to extend the coast. But such gains are temporary, for gnawing waves, subsidence of the land, and at times rising sea levels inexorably shrink the islands. Older lava islands, such as Kure and Midway at the northwestern end of the chain, keep their heads above water only because of thick caps of growing coral.

Some of the powerful waves that pound the Hawaiian Islands originate thousands of miles away. Winter storms, sweeping eastward from Siberia, produce huge swells that roll unchecked across the Pacific. Below the Equator, summer storms can generate equally awesome swells.

Offshore, the ocean swells strike fringing coral reefs and shallow bottom areas of rocks or sand. Slowed, the swells bulge upward into towering rollers, giant waves that lure surfers from around the world. The best come to challenge waves more than 30 feet high at Oahu's Makaha, Waimea, and Sunset Beaches.

Ocean waves that fetch disaster to Hawaii are the tsunamis. Triggered by earthquakes as far away as South America, these seismic waves at times strike the islands with silent doom. In May of 1960 a tsunami of three major and numerous smaller waves—including a 35-foot wall of water that partially destroyed Hilo, on the Big Island—killed 61 people.

Hawaii's earliest inhabitants, emigrants from other Polynesian isles, knew well the power of the sea. Yet they also knew its bounty. They relied heavily on the sea for food, building ingenious holding ponds for their catch in the lava rocks along the shore.

Because of prevailing currents and temperature patterns, most of Hawaii's fishes migrated from Indonesia or Southeast Asia. Some 600 species swim these waters, ranging from giant sharks to the little fish whose name may exceed its length, the *humuhumunukunukuapua'a*.

Marine mammals also spend parts of the year in the archipelago. In winter several hundred humpback whales travel here from summer feeding grounds in colder waters. Many cavort in the blue depths near Maui and Hawaii. Swimming just offshore, the majestic animals symbolize the enduring splendor of the islands.

Waves lap grainy lava of Black Sand Beach on Hawaii, largest of the eight principal islands in the chain. Throughout the archipelago, relentless waves grind away at lava and coral.

FOLLOWING PAGES: Strollers watch seas explode against a lava ledge at Hanauma Bay on Oahu.

PAGES 188-89: Humpback cow and calf swim the indigo waters of Hawaii. Each winter, humpbacks migrate here to calve and to compete for mates.

PAUL CHESLEY. FOLLOWING PAGES: PETER FRENCH
PAGES 188-89: FLIP NICKLIN/NICKLIN & ASSOCIATES

Alaska

THE EARTHQUAKE STRUCK with terrible swiftness. In an instant on the afternoon of March 27, 1964, a 500-mile stretch of Alaska's southern coast was rocked by a force equal to thousands of atomic blasts. It was the strongest North American quake on record in this century.

The '64 quake, however, was unique only in its magnitude. Along this part of the volcano-spattered Ring of Fire, earthquakes are triggered often as plates of earth's crust jostle and one slides beneath the other. Alaska itself was born of such violence. Recent studies suggest Alaska is a patchwork of some 50 terranes, remnants of ancient landforms scraped from moving plates and rammed together over the past 150 million years.

Alaska's tortuous shoreline reflects the latest phase of that complex earth history. Around the southern rim such forces have thrust up the Chugach and St. Elias ranges—as well as the Aleutian Islands and the craggy Alaska Peninsula, which are dotted with active volcanoes. But what shifting plates upraise, glaciers and weathering work to wear down. In the Alexander Archipelago, a maze of some 11,000 islands, glaciers have carved deep valleys. Some have subsided under the sea to become fjords.

The sum of this geological inheritance is a coastline staggering in its diversity. Contrasted with lushly forested islands of the southeastern archipelago are treeless, cliff-cut coastal plains along the Arctic Ocean; in western Alaska sandy or muddy shores alternate with forbidding cliffs that brood over the Bering Sea.

Throughout these coastal zones, plentiful wildlife sustained indigenous cultures. Long before Vitus Bering sighted Alaska in 1741, native people harvested fish and hunted whales and seals. To some extent, they still do.

The interplay of wildlife, water, and land is constant here. Tidewater glaciers calve icebergs on which seals haul out to birth their young. Lumbering brown bears seek seafood and easy thoroughfares along gravelly shores. Noisy gulls share rocky perches with basking sea lions. Millions of migratory birds breed along the coast.

These and other animals thrive thanks to the seasonal bounty of food in Alaska's coastal waters. Through the breeding season seabird colonies exploit rich stocks of fish. Baleen whales, such as the humpback, return each year to gorge on enormous quantities of shrimplike krill.

A long, harsh winter cordons many areas of the coast. Ice blocks western and northern shores for three-quarters of the year or more, and fierce storms wrack the Aleutian Islands. In the southeast more moderate temperatures prevail.

In all seasons Alaska's shores are awesome, a wild, breathtaking expanse. And, like the wilderness interior, much of the coast is protected, knit by a succession of national parks, forests, monuments, preserves, and wildlife refuges.

From Misty Fjords National Monument in the southeast to the Arctic National Wildlife Refuge in the far north, this vast land adds a distinctive patch to the American mosaic, as different as Hawaii's roller coaster surf, California's hypnotic kelp forests, Louisiana's labyrinthine delta lands, or Florida's mangrove-fringed keys. Indeed, each of these areas bears an unmatched quality, an abiding uniqueness that enchants all who wander the restless domain where the land meets the sea.

Emblem of a fiery past, a 100-foot-high dike cuts through darker volcanic rock in the Aleutians. The dike, formed as molten rock, penetrated a fissure.

FOLLOWING PAGES: Harbor seals rest on ice floes at the foot of Le Conte Glacier in the Alexander Archipelago. A wealth of wildlife thrives on the food produced in fertile Alaskan waters.

PAGES 194-95: Volcanic Augustine Island, its dome lost in clouds, rises off the Alaska Peninsula.

STEVEN C. WILSON/ENTHEOS. FOLLOWING PAGES: TOM BEAN.
PAGES 194-95: J & M IBBOTSON/APERTURE PHOTOBANK

Notes on Contributors
Tom Melham, H. Robert Morrison, Cynthia Russ Ramsay, and Suzanne Venino are staff writers in the Special Publications Division. Wheeler J. North is professor of environmental science at the California Institute of Technology. Free-lance photographers Matt Bradley, Stephen J. Krasemann, and Tim Thompson have contributed to numerous Society publications. Photographer Stephen Frink is an underwater specialist based in Florida.

Acknowledgments
The years do little to dispel the magic of Rachel Carson's writing; its potency is evident in this book. We gratefully acknowledge the sources of the quotations in the introduction and preceding the major chapters as follows: Page 10, from *The Sea Around Us*, pages 119, 120. Copyright © 1950, 1951, 1961 by Rachel L. Carson; renewed 1979 by Roger Christie. Reprinted by permission of Oxford University Press, Inc., Frances Collin, Literary Trustee. Pages 9, 44, 80, and 146, from *The Edge of the Sea*, pages 249-50, 130, 125, and 27. Copyright © 1955 by Rachel L. Carson; renewed 1983 by Roger Christie. Reprinted by permission of Houghton Mifflin Company, Frances Collin, Literary Trustee. Page 116, from "Mattamuskeet," *Conservation in Action*, U.S. Department of the Interior, Copyright © 1947.

Throughout the course of this project the staff enjoyed the cooperation of the men and women of the state coastal management offices. Specialists at the National Marine Fisheries Service, National Oceanic and Atmospheric Administration, National Park Service, Smithsonian Institution, U.S. Fish and Wildlife Service, and U.S. Geological Survey helped with points of detail. Many individuals who assisted us are cited in the book; in addition special thanks are owed to the following: For help throughout the book, Franklin D. Christhilf, William V. Sliter, Alexander Sprunt IV.

We also wish to express our gratitude to consultants who gave generously of their time and expertise in each chapter: *Pacific chapters*—Willard Bascom, Michael A. Bigg, Jim Darling, Michael S. Foster, William E. McIntyre, Donald J. Usner. *Gulf of Mexico chapter*—Billy D. Causey, John Halas, Henry Hildebrand, Robert J. Misso, Darlene Taylor, Kris Thoemke. *Atlantic chapters*—James Allen, George C. Baker, Scott Brumburgh, Peter Burn, Michael Burzynski, Richard Crlenjak, Jean Evoy, Nathan M. Frohling, Albert Hinn, Peter F. Larsen, Charles A. Oravetz, David Rutherford, Ricky W. Schechtman, Barbara Vickery, John Page Williams. *Virgin Islands, Hawaii, and Alaska portfolios*—William DeCreeft, R.W. Grigg, Lawrence Guth, Steve Nelson, Bruce Reed, Gary Winkler.

Additional Reading
We gained inspiration, insight, and information from Miss Carson's works. We referred often to articles in National Geographic and to other Society publications; check the cumulative index. Articles in the periodical *Oceans* also proved helpful. And among the many books we consulted, we found the following particularly useful: Willard Bascom, *Waves and Beaches*; Michael and Deborah Berrill, *A Sierra Club Naturalist's Guide to the North Atlantic Coast*; Thomas Carefoot, *Pacific Seashores*; Coast Alliance, *Coast Alert*; E. Yale Dawson and Michael S. Foster, *Seashore Plants of California*; Ben R. Finney and James D. Houston, *Surfing*; Nick Fotheringham, *Beachcomber's Guide to Gulf Coast Marine Life*; William T. Fox, *At the Sea's Edge*; Kenneth L. Gosner, *A Field Guide to the Atlantic Seashore*; George H. Harrison, *Roger Tory Peterson's Dozen Birding Hot Spots*; Eugene H. Kaplan, *A Field Guide to Coral Reefs*; Wallace Kaufman and Orrin Pilkey, *The Beaches are Moving*; James P. Kennett, *Marine Geology*; Norman A. Meinkoth, *Audubon Society Guide to North American Seashore Creatures*; Anne W. Simon, *The Thin Edge*; H.U. Sverdrup, *The Oceans*; John and Mildred Teal, *Life and Death of the Salt Marsh*.

JACK DERMID

Not yet fledged, the summer's crop of young royal terns strolls the beach of a breeding colony in the Cape Fear River estuary, North Carolina.

Library of Congress CIP Data
Main entry under title:

America's seashore wonderlands.

  Bibliography: p.
  Includes index.
  1. Seashore ecology—North America. I. National Geographic Society (U.S.). Special Publications Division.
QH102.A54   1985   574.5'2638'097   85-25848
ISBN 0-87044-543-X (regular edition)
ISBN 0-87044-548-0 (library edition)

Composition for *America's Seashore Wonderlands* by National Geographic's Photographic Services, Carl M. Shrader, Director, Lawrence F. Ludwig, Assistant Director. Printed and bound by Holladay-Tyler Printing Corp., Rockville, Md. Film preparation by Catharine Cooke Studio, Inc., New York, N.Y. Color separations by the Lanman Progressive Company, Washington, D.C.; Lincoln Graphics, Inc., Cherry Hill N.J.; and NEC, Inc., Nashville, Tenn.

Index